Famous Biographies for Young People

FAMOUS BLACK
ENTERTAINERS
OF TODAY

OTHER BOOKS BY RAOUL ABDUL

The Magic of Black Poetry
Three Thousand Years of Black Poetry
(with Alan Lomax)

FAMOUS BLACK
ENTERTAINERS
OF TODAY

by Raoul Abdul

ILLUSTRATED WITH PHOTOGRAPHS

Dodd, Mead & Company · New York

ACKNOWLEDGMENT

THE AUTHOR wishes to thank Richard M. Haber for his assistance in preparing the manuscript of this book.

The review by Emory Lewis is reproduced by his permission.

ISBN: 0-396-06849-9
Library of Congress Catalog Card Number: 73-7096
Printed in the United States of America
by Vail-Ballou Press, Inc., Binghamton, N.Y.

TO RUSSELL AND ROWENA JELLIFFE
founders of Karamu Theatre
where so many gifted young people have
found themselves through participation
in the arts.

CONTENTS

Illustrations follow page 80

CONTENTS

INTRODUCTION

During the last decade, a new kind of black personality has emerged on the entertainment scene. He has shattered many of the old stereotypes and created a new image of black people in dance, music, theatre, film, and television. Each season, outstanding new talents appear in the galaxy like fireworks on the Fourth of July only to explode into a magnificent display and then quickly disappear into oblivion. But some of these personalities manage to endure, and it is from this group that I have chosen eighteen to *represent* America's great reservoir of black talent.

The dance and musical traditions of black Americans go back to Africa where they were an integral part of the daily lives of all of the people. There were dances and songs to celebrate all of the special events of the life cycle from birth to death. In spite of the fact that blacks were removed from the land of their roots, these cultural ties remained unbroken. Now, of course, there has been a *fusion* of black and white cultural traditions which has resulted in something uniquely *American*.

Born from this fusion of cultural traditions are two of America's leading dance companies, The Alvin Ailey City Center Dance Theater and Dance Theatre of Harlem, founded by Alvin Ailey and Arthur Mitchell respectively.

In succeeding chapters, each of these distinguished young men will speak of his work in his own words. But first, tribute must be paid to those pioneers who paved the way.

One of the earliest serious black dance companies appeared on April 29, 1931, at the Theatre-in-the-Clouds atop the Chanin Building in New York City. It was called the New Negro Art Theatre, and its guiding light was Hemsley Winfield. Several years later, Winfield and his dancers were engaged to perform in an operatic version of *The Emperor Jones* given by the Metropolitan Opera. Another important group, the American Negro Ballet Group, came into being in 1935 under the direction of Eugene Von Grona. An important pioneer in the area of ethnic dance was Pearl Primus, who went to Africa and studied firsthand West African folk materials and incorporated them into formal pieces for her company. From time to time, many fine groups made impressive beginnings, but were unable to get the kind of financial backing necessary to stay together on a permanent basis.

The one exception was Katherine Dunham, who managed for over twenty years to keep her company working. Miss Dunham first came to New York in 1940 with a concert of American and Caribbean dances of which Arthur Todd of *The New York Times* wrote: ". . . her sense of rhythm, theatre and costuming and her wonderful performers—as well as her choreography and dancing—put serious Negro dance on the map once and for all." Indeed, the Dunham dancers conquered the world with their magnificent performances. Out of Miss Dunham's company and school came some of the brightest stars of the current scene.

In the field of classical ballet, mention must be made of Janet Collins, who became the first black prima ballerina when she was engaged by the Metropolitan Opera for the 1951–52 season. Miss Collins's struggle to make a place for herself in ballet and her eventual triumph is the stuff on which a fascinating novel might be based. It was Miss Collins who paved the way for Arthur Mitchell, who, since his debut with the New York City Ballet in 1955, rose to become the world's most celebrated black premier danseur.

Much has been written about the black contribution to American music, particularly that which is deeply rooted in ethnic tradition. This includes the Spirituals, the Blues, Ragtime, Gospel, Jazz, and Rhythm and Blues. The basic beat which was first heard in Africa has continued to pound with such insistence that it has left its imprint on the musical fabric of the entire Western world. It should not be forgotten that the American popular song form was moulded out of a fusion of Afro-American and Euro-American elements, a fact which many people still refuse to acknowledge.

Black America has its own special Oscar which it bestows upon its most beloved performers of popular music. Today's "Queen of Soul" Aretha Franklin is descended from a long line of singing royalty starting with "Ma" Rainey, who was called "Mother of the Blues." Her successor was Bessie Smith, "Empress of the Blues." Billie Holiday was called "Lady Day;" Dinah Washington, "Queen of the Blues;" Sarah Vaughn, "The Divine Sarah." Even though he has not yet been given a title, gospel singer Alex Bradford can trace his musical heritage back to Dr. Thomas A.

Dorsey, "Father of the Gospel Song." Diana Ross proved with her remarkable performance in *Lady Sings the Blues* that she has been touched by the magic of "Lady Day." Critic-composer Carman Moore makes us aware of those who are keeping the black musical traditions alive through his reviews in *The New York Times* and *The Village Voice*.

A large number of black musicians have chosen to specialize in the area of European classical music, and it is unfortunate that so little has been written about them. How many people know of the great violinist George Bridgetower (1789–1860) for whom Beethoven wrote his celebrated Kreutzer Sonata? Born in Poland of an African father and European mother, he was a favorite in the highest musical circles of Europe. Another violin virtuoso was Cuban-born Joseph White (1833–1920). Although Europe was the scene of most of his triumphs, White did play in the United States (Boston and New York) in 1876. Also a composer, his violin concerto has recently been revived by the Symphony of the New World in New York City.

Included in this book are opera singer Martina Arroyo, symphonic conductor James DePriest, and concert pianist André Watts. A leading soprano at the Metropolitan Opera, Miss Arroyo treads a path cleared by Katerina Jarboro in 1933 when she became the first black to appear in a leading role with a major American opera company. She played Aïda at the Chicago Opera. The doors of the Metropolitan Opera were opened to blacks by contralto Marian Anderson, who made her debut there in 1955 in Verdi's *The Masked Ball*. Paving the way for James DePriest was Dean Dixon, the first of his race to devote his entire career to symphonic conducting. Before it was possible for André Watts to dazzle the musical world with his spectacular debut with the New York Philharmonic in 1963, it took the pioneering efforts of Busoni's black student Hazel Harrison of a previous generation and Natalie Hinderas, who was one of the first black pianists to be accepted by a major management. Hinderas is only now receiving the kind of recognition her remarkable talent deserves.

Until recently, there used to be sharp lines drawn between people working in theatre (musical or dramatic), film, and television. The key word now is versatility. Gloria Foster, Micki Grant, James Earl Jones, Ben Vereen, and Melvin Van Peebles seem at home in each media. Ms. Grant has expanded her activities with great success to include writing songs and lyrics. Van Peebles has explored the gamut from writing through producing and distributing. Flip Wilson gives the impression that he has some hidden aces in his deck of theatrical cards which may help him to expand beyond television and nightclubs. Producer Ellis Haizlip has proven his versatility by working in television, on the legitimate stage, and in the concert hall.

These young people have a remarkable heritage from which to draw inspiration. While many black Americans were still enslaved, Ira Aldridge (1807–1867) was thrilling audiences in England, continental Europe, and Russia with his appearances in *Othello, The Merchant of Venice,* and *Macbeth.* In 1920, Charles Gilpin played the title role in Eugene O'Neill's *The Emperor Jones.* Other outstanding performers who made theatrical history were: Rose McClendon in Paul Green's *In Abraham's Bosom* (1926); Frank Wilson in Dorothy and Du Bose Heyward's *Porgy* (1927);

Richard B. Harrison in *The Green Pastures* (1930); and Paul Robeson in *Othello* (1943), which set a record for the longest run of a Shakespearean play on Broadway. The first black playwright to reach Broadway with a full-length play was Garland Anderson, whose *Appearances* opened in 1925. Sissle and Blake heralded a decade of black musicals when *Shuffle Along* was produced in 1921. From these musicals emerged such great talents as Burt Williams, who became the first black star of the *Ziegfeld Follies;* Florence Mills, who became an international favorite in her short lifetime; and Josephine Baker, who is still one of the world's greatest entertainers.

When Sidney Poitier accepted the Academy Award as best male actor in 1963 for his performance in *Lilies of the Field,* he said rightfully: "It has been a long journey to this moment." The journey of which he spoke began in 1903 when Edwin S. Porter's *Uncle Tom's Cabin* introduced to film its first black character—"Uncle Tom." Thomas Alva Edison not only invented the electric bulb, but also the classic "Coon," when he produced *Ten Pickaninnies* in 1904. The "Tragic Mulatto" began to appear in such movies as *The Debt* in 1912. "Mammy," as seen in *Coon Town Suffragettes* (1914), reached her zenith in the person of Hattie McDaniel when she was awarded the Academy Award for *Gone with the Wind* in 1939. The "Brutal Black Buck" was introduced in D.W. Griffith's *The Birth of a Nation* in 1915. These stereotypes, set so firmly at the beginning of the film industry, have continued to exist with only a few notable exceptions to the present day. This has been documented in Donald Bogle's extraordinary book *Toms, Coons, Mulattoes, Mammies & Bucks,* an interpretative history of blacks in American films.

When Melvin Van Peebles' *The Story of a Three-Day Pass* opened in New York in 1968, *The New York Times* critic Renata Adler claimed that he was "the first American Negro director of a film of feature length." Because so little had been done by way of scholarship in the area of blacks in film, Ms. Adler could not be blamed for having no knowledge of the films of such black filmmakers as Oscar Micheaux. From *The Homesteader* (1919) to *The Betrayal* (1948), Micheaux produced thirty-four pictures. His actors included such names as Lorenzo Tucker, "the black Valentino" and Bee Freeman, "the Sepia Mae West." In the chapters of this volume on Van Peebles, Ron O'Neal, and Cicely Tyson, the reader will see how each of these young people has come to grips with this heritage.

In the early days of television, black viewers were so starved for images with which they could identify that they reluctantly accepted an all-black series entitled "Amos 'n' Andy," brought to CBS in 1951. It turned out to be a video version of the same old stereotypes perpetuated for over a quarter of a century on the original radio series. The NAACP finally persuaded the network to discontinue it in 1957. Despite opposition from the Southern market, Ed Sullivan insisted on presenting top black variety artists on his long-running "The Ed Sullivan Show," which began on CBS in 1948. Soon after, other important shows followed his example.

It was not until 1957 that a major network presented a black performer in his own series. NBC ran the "Nat 'King' Cole Show" for several months until it was apparent that sponsors were not ready yet to take a chance on a black program. When Bill Cosby became the first black co-star of a continuing series (with Robert Culp) entitled "I Spy," the show met with extraordinary success and he personally received an Emmy as Best Dramatic Actor in 1965. Another milestone was when Harry Belafonte became the first black to produce a major TV special in 1966—"The Strollin' Twenties" (CBS).

Now, it is no longer unsual to see blacks being utilized in a dignified manner on commercials, newscasts, daytime serials, children's shows, variety shows, and dramatic presentations. The spectacular success of "The Flip Wilson Show," which, since its debut on NBC in 1970, has maintained the highest ratings, has proved that black can be box-office magic. And Ellis Haizlip's "Soul!" series on the P.B.S. network has shown that even a program that is addressed exclusively to the black community can be a great success.

—Raoul Abdul

FAMOUS BLACK
ENTERTAINERS
OF TODAY

ALVIN AILEY

Director, Alvin Ailey City Center Dance Theater

TEXAS-BORN Alvin Ailey has seen his company, The Alvin Ailey City Center Dance Theater, rise from an unknown group making its debut at the YMHA in 1958 to the position of one of the world's greatest. Its international tours have taken the company to six continents and every major country including the Soviet Union. Besides choreographing for his own company, Ailey created the dances for Samuel Barber's opera *Anthony and Cleopatra* which opened the new Metropolitan Opera House, as well as the new production of *Carmen.* He also choreographed and collaborated in the staging of Leonard Bernstein's *Mass,* which officially opened the John F. Kennedy Center for the Performing Arts in Washington, D.C. Ailey holds honorary degrees from both Cedar Crest College and Princeton University. The following conversation took place in his school, The American Dance Center.

ABDUL: Why do you think that there is such a large audience for dance today?

AILEY: With the help of the Arts Council and the National Foundation for the Arts, there's been a great profusion of companies. It's been more readily available, so the

21

kids have been able to see it more and have been able to understand that it's something that is a part of everyday life.

ABDUL: Do you think that those festivals such as the ones at Bennington and Connecticut have had some influence?

AILEY: There's a lot of dance in the colleges now, and all those places like Bennington and Connecticut have turned out teachers who have gone out and spread the word.

ABDUL: Since you had a long career as a dancer yourself, how does it feel to look up on the stage and see your dancers doing all those things you used to do? Don't you want to jump up on stage and start all over again?

AILEY: No. I never look back. I stopped dancing in 1965. I made up my mind one morning and said: "This is it!" I put all the dance belts, shoes, tights, and T-shirts into a wastebasket in Florence, Italy. I'll never forget it.

ABDUL: Was this with your own company?

AILEY: Yes. It was the end of a nine-month tour—the first time we went to Europe.

ABDUL: I see that your company has just become a part of New York City Center, so it will have a permanent home.

AILEY: Which doesn't mean that we won't have any problems, you know. We still have the same old problems with money, but now we have a large board and they're starting to do something, but you just live in debt.

ABDUL: Well, you've managed to survive.

AILEY: We survive mainly by working. For a long time people thought that we were heavily subsidized—they are always saying that we're rich because we always look good on stage, they always see our name around, and we're always going hither, thither, and yon—but we don't have any money. We came into existence in 1958, but until the Arts Council started giving out bread, we were never given any money. We toured and we always paid our own expenses by what we made from touring, which is unheard of. We could tour fifty-two weeks a year, but the kids just couldn't take it.

ABDUL: Well, they wouldn't have a chance to learn new things.

AILEY: They don't feel that they're dancing well when they're doing so many performances a week. But still we have to tour in order to survive. It's the old story, but it's been made better recently by the National Endowment. They pay schools a third of your fee. It's a residency program. We go into university areas and stay there a few days. We do classes on campus and give lecture demonstrations and finally end up by giving one or two performances, which is good, because it keeps the kids in one place for a while.

ABDUL: What you are really doing is building audiences and inspiring future Alvin Aileys.

AILEY: I don't know how many. If they only knew all the problems—but it's getting a little bit better. There are a lot of young companies around now.

ABDUL: You wonder how they can survive because there are so many.

AILEY: When they don't have money to rehearse, they break up. They lose dancers and lose their "rep" and when they do get a little bit of money, they have to start all over again to teach new people.

ABDUL: When did you first start dancing yourself?

AILEY: In 1949 between high school and college. Sometime around that time—I had known Carmen De Lavallade—we went to the same junior high. There were some mad people around the school who danced—and it was *quite* a mad thing to be doing in *those* days.

ABDUL: Did they have a particularly good arts program there?

AILEY: No, but the way I did come on dance was through a junior high school teacher. He took students on Saturday expeditions to the middle of Los Angeles. We'd go to the Philharmonic Hall or the Biltmore Theatre—these cultural events—and one of the things I went to see was the Ballet Russe. I was very impressed by it. But more important, it served to introduce me to where the theatre area in Los Angeles was. I lived in the ghetto, you know.

ABDUL: Which meant that you seldom went outside of that area.

AILEY: Yes. So when I got down there, then I knew where everything was. I said: "Oh, my God—look at this—this is the whole world!" So, I used to hang out down there after I had gone to those Saturday matinees. One day at the Biltmore there was an advertisement for a black company—Katherine Dunham. This was in 1945, I'll never forget. I saw Miss Dunham. That was the big thing—I knew that black people could dance when I saw it. In the 1940s, you only saw black people doing tap dancing on the screen in films like *Cabin in the Sky* and *Stormy Weather*.

ABDUL: Did you go backstage and meet the dancers?

AILEY: I was one of those kids who'd hang around the

24

stage door, and there was a friend of mine named Ted Crumm who lived around the corner from me. He had actually been out to the Lester Horton Studio and he was very hip to the Dunham thing. I met him outside the stage door of the Dunham's. One of the Dunham company started giving lessons at a nightclub in the black section—it was called the Dewdrop Inn or Ivory Pearl—one of those things. I went to a couple of classes—that was the first time I ever danced.

ABDUL: Did that lead to further study?

AILEY: Then I went to Lester Horton. Carmen De Lavallade was going there and Ted was going there and I saw modern dance for the first time—it freaked me out. So, between high school and college, I went out to the Lester Horton Studio and studied for three or four months— then went away and came back.

ABDUL: What did you study at college?

AILEY: I was studying romance languages. I only went to college for two years because the dance pull got very strong.

ABDUL: So, what happened?

AILEY: It was very difficult running back and forth between the ghetto and Los Angeles and U.C.L.A. It was two hours away, so I had very little time to study, but Lester was very nice. He called me up one day after I had disappeared from classes and said, "What happened to you?" I told him I was going to school and couldn't study dance. So, he said, "I think you can probably be a dancer if you really want to be a dancer." At that time I was eighteen. He said, "Why don't you just come whenever you can." They were doing two seasons a year—on Friday and Saturday nights—so, I sort of became associated with the Horton Studio. Carmen was there and Jimmy Truett and Ted were there—so that really kind of opened my eyes to what dancing was all about.

ABDUL: Was Lester Horton black?

AILEY: No, but he was very interested in all forms, all cultures—very immersed in the Orient, in the American Indian, in blacks—immersed in all kinds of music. It was just a wide-open place.

ABDUL: It must have been a wonderful place in which to develop.

AILEY: When Lester died in 1953, they needed a choreographer. It was decided that we were all supposed to submit a scenario, but when the time came, nobody presented anything but me. So, I started doing the first choreography there—for the Horton Company. We came to Jacob's Pillow in the summer of 1954 because the company had an engagement there. And we did some auditions. Lester had some Latin American dances that were rather commercial which we used to dance at nightclubs. They were called "work dances," because we could make money doing them on television and in clubs. We were showing these dances to some television people at the Alvin Theatre in New York where, at the same time, they were auditioning "House of Flowers." Eventually we did that show. We said that we would stay for six months in New York and then go back to California.

ABDUL: And you ended up staying in New York permanently.

AILEY: After "House of Flowers," I decided to stay in New York and study. I studied with everybody who was around including Karel Shook. He was one of the few ballet teachers who really welcomed black dancers. He had a little studio on Eighth Avenue and Forty-fifth Street above a shop. He was a philosopher, too. He used to call people up and say, "Get to class this morning! If you are serious about dancing, get to class!"

ABDUL: He sounds like a good disciplinarian.

AILEY: The very essence of dance is discipline—you cannot be a fine dancer without discipline.

ABDUL: Well, it's obvious that you have very good discipline in your company.

AILEY: I don't take people who are undisciplined unless they are just madly talented. I choose people for talent mainly, and if you have to wrangle with a personality to get them to do what you think they should do, then you do it. Dancing is very difficult—a dancer has to know that he wants to dance—it is not something you come to play with. Once the bug has bitten you, then discipline is a part of your life. So, anybody who can't accept these things cannot be a dancer.

ABDUL: What plans have you for the future of the Alvin Ailey City Center Dance Theater?

AILEY: Well, I want to get better facilities and what I want to develop around here is the kind of attitude that Lester Horton had at his school. Lester made you feel that the arts were a part of your normal life—that dancers, painters, and singers were not something special—but it was just a part of your natural expression. And that's the kind of thing I'd like in our company, too. I don't like people who feel that they're very "up" because they're a dancer. Dance is simply a gift that you've been given—you are meant to do that. I want to go on developing a repertory. I want to develop the Katherine Dunham repertory in the company and the works of other black artists who are no longer doing their thing. And I'm trying to develop choreographers within the company.

ABDUL: Is there any particular reason why your company is integrated?

AILEY: It's a big family, this company. It's kind of like the family of man. It gives me special pleasure when all those children come downstage at the end of a performance—eight black ones and four white ones—and the audience is applauding for *everybody*. And whether they know it or not, they are applauding the idea that people should get together.

MARTINA ARROYO
International Opera Star

IT WOULD take a round-the-world trip to keep up with Harlem-born soprano Martina Arroyo. If you miss her at New York's Metropolitan Opera, you might catch up with her in Milan at La Scala, in London at Covent Garden, in Vienna at the Staatsoper, or in Buenos Aires at the Teatro Colón. Or, you might find her singing with the Cleveland Orchestra, Boston Symphony, or even as Johnny Carson's guest on "The Tonight Show." Wherever she is, you can be sure of one thing—she will be the prima donna (an operatic term for first lady or star). The following conversation took place in Miss Arroyo's seven-room apartment on Manhattan's East Side, where she spoke of her life, her career, and her advice to young people who think they might like to have a musical career.

ARROYO: Actually, you were in on the very beginning of my career because, when I met you, I was doing a concert in Vienna for Amerika-Haus. That's how I got started— singing lieder and oratorio. I think that this has had an influence on my life as an opera singer because I never got out of the sincere affection for lieder and oratorio. It is still part of the career. This means that I pull out of the opera scene, and I think that it keeps the voice fresh and keeps me in contact with another musical form which is extremely important because it is more intimate.

ABDUL: A lieder concert is like creating eighteen different roles on one program, isn't it?

ARROYO: Right. And each one will influence the other. You try to bring something from your lieder approach into the opera. But it's not very easy, because opera is done on such a grand scale. Distance also makes a difference. And, of course, the effect one colleague has on another plays its part. But you try anyway and consider it ideal if it can be done that way.

ABDUL: Did you ever study acting?

ARROYO: I started my training that way in the opera workshop at Hunter College under Josef Turnau. He is the one who really became interested. He sent me to my singing teacher. He got the scholarship for me.

ABDUL: Who is your teacher?

ARROYO: Marinka Gurevich, an incredible lady.

ABDUL: What is the day in the life of an opera singer like? For example, a day on which you have to sing?

ARROYO: That's the one nice day, because I get to sleep in the afternoon. On the other days, you are racing around getting your hair done, you go to fittings, you go to rehearsals, you have to study, grab planes, take an interview between your flight and lunch. Or you might have to go for a photo session which might take six hours.

ABDUL: How do you feel about the black singer in relationship to the kinds of roles he can play?

ARROYO: First of all, to me being black is not a problem. You simply have to know more about makeup as any good stage person must. I've sat down with Elinor Ross, who is as lily-white as the day is long, and our problems were very similar. Not black or white. Our problems were: What can you do with this round face? What can you do with these big eyes, especially with your mouth open singing? What can you do with makeup, with costumes, to create the image? How can you use *your* qualities for the character-ization and make it work? That's a problem that is not a black problem, but rather one which every one of us has.

ABDUL: One of the roles you have played at the Metro-politan Opera is Elsa in *Lohengrin.* And Elsa is the symbol of white womanhood.

ARROYO: For many people it came as a shock that Elsa worked better for me than many of the so-called "black" roles. Some people thought Mr. Bing [then General Direc-tor of the Met] had lost his mind. Of course, the Wieland Wagner production didn't allow for very much move-ment—it's a highly stylized thing. But Mr. Bing went with me to the dressmaking department and tried the costumes on me and made the slight changes that made all the dif-ference in the world. Instead of putting me in white and *silver,* he put me in white and *gold.* It still gave the so-called "white" look, but with the gold hues with my soft-toned skin, I gave the same impression which wouldn't have worked for me with the silver. It just took a bit of extra thinking and came out with the same results. They would have had that same problem with Gabriela Tucci because she is dark.

ABDUL: How did the critics react?

ARROYO: It was probably one of the biggest successes I've had at the Met besides Lady Macbeth, which I think is my biggest success.

31

ABDUL: For my taste *Macbeth* as an opera is a greater piece of theatre than the play. I know that it's sacrilege to say it.

ARROYO: No, it isn't. I am terribly interested in that opera and loved doing it. I started studying that opera by going to see the stage version to see various approaches to the role of Lady Macbeth.

ABDUL: Have you worked with directors from the legitimate theatre?

ARROYO: Last year at the San Francisco Opera I did *The Masked Ball* with an actor as stage director. He did some things that were absolutely incredible.

ABDUL: What happens when you learn a role with a director at one house and then find yourself having to play it somewhere else with another director?

ARROYO: A lot will depend on your colleagues—what types of people you're working with. In fact, it did happen. Shortly afterward I went to work in Chicago with another fine actor, but not a theatre man—Tito Gobbi. He knows how to make theatre work for him and I was very interested in trying to see how he did it, but he can't teach. He just did it and it was always right. So, I found myself going back and employing some of the things I had learned from the San Francisco production because that characterization had come from myself. And that was interesting. One of the colleagues in this particular production was Sherrill Milnes, who is the type of man with whom you *can* work. So, by employing some of those ideas with Sherrill, it worked even better than in the San Francisco production.

ABDUL: The role of Amelia in *The Masked Ball* is a great

role for you.

ARROYO: I love it. I'm not trying to knock any of my other colleagues, but when you see someone like a Sherrill Milnes really work out a scene—and we really worked—and Riri Grist. She was Oscar, the page. We had one rehearsal when the director tried to say something and we said, "Shh!" because we were working so intensely, and I said, "Oh, my goodness, I'm sorry." What happened was that each of us was reacting so beautifully together that we got carried away.

ABDUL: It must be very interesting to work on the same material with different people at different times and places.

ARROYO: Surely. That's the whole key to it. And, without rehearsal you can't make it work. Riri Grist is also one of those very hard workers. She knows so much about the stage. She's got it right at her fingertips. Placido Domingo, the tenor, is another *working* colleague. When we worked together, the performance made sense. When you don't have these types of colleagues, all you get is the old-style opera.

ABDUL: The younger opera singers are more theatre oriented.

ARROYO: So is the audience, isn't it?

ABDUL: What would you suggest to the young person who feels he has a talent for singing and would like to develop it?

ARROYO: It depends on what you mean by young. You have to be very careful that you don't hurt the voice before it matures. Of course, your choice of teachers is the biggest problem of your entire career. If the voice has not yet reached maturity, I would suggest the study of a string instrument and the piano. The string instrument helps in training the ear, in the learning of intervals. If the person has the time, I would start that way. Then, get as much repertoire as you can—listening to all kinds of music and going to concerts. And don't leave out popular music. You can get some of the most beautiful phrasing in the world from listening to Roberta Flack. Another thing is not to sing the wrong things too early. Allow the voice to grow naturally. Start learning old Italian songs and lieder. Learn about line, about legato. You can learn these things before the voice matures because what you will be doing is developing it and helping it to grow without pushing. You can push a voice in the wrong direction and ruin a good instrument. You can learn your languages, the music, and learn about the characters in opera.

ABDUL: Is there any problem of adjustment when a singer rises from modest circumstances to a postition of stardom?

ARROYO: It depends on how free you are. The fact that one comes from a poor economic situation does not mean that the things one has are not good. Most of the furniture you see in this apartment, which is an enormous one containing seven rooms, is from our place on 111th Street. We always had lovely things and still have them. We have a few new pieces, certainly. It is nicer now that we have a beautiful grand instead of an upright piano. But that has less meaning in this house than many of the other pieces we brought with us. The nicest pieces in the world are those acquired when you are just being able to afford to go out and buy them and you say, "No, I have to put that fifteen dollars a month aside for that piano." That upright piano meant so much to me that I couldn't bear to get rid of it. So, I finally gave it to my girlfriend's daughter, who is now studying on it and who adores it as much as I did. It has meaning for her. Another thing is that you should keep your mind free and don't worry about being black. That's no problem—it's a simple fact—like you are a man or a woman or tall or short. It's not a problem being that thing. Just let it be and don't try to change it. If you try to be something else, then you are in trouble. Know yourself— you have to know what you are.

ABDUL: What do you do when you have a little spare time for yourself?

ARROYO: Well, last week I went to Puerto Rico and got an infection from mosquitoes, which caused me to have to cancel a performance. Next time I'll stay home and work.

ABDUL: Do you watch television at all?

ARROYO: I love it. As a media, it could be a great source of information and strength in the home.

ABDUL: Some people call it "The Idiot Box."

ARROYO: It doesn't have to be. You must be selective, that's all. You can see such things as Nureyev and Fontaine. And, I saw *The Masked Ball* from Sweden. Can you imagine what it's like to bring opera close up so people can see the development of the characters right in your own home? And, I've seen some wonderful old movies which I could not have seen when they originally came out because I was too young. What young people today have at their disposal is so incredible. You can be like a sponge and soak all of this up or you can let it keep you from growing if you let it. But, I'd love to be fifteen again and be starting out with all these resources at my disposal.

ALEX BRADFORD

Gospel Singer - Composer

AT THE AGE of thirteen in his native Bessemer, Alabama, Alex Bradford decided to devote his life to gospel
music. Now, he is one of the world's foremost exponents
of that lively musical form. As one of the stars of Langston
Hughes's gospel song-play *Black Nativity,* Bradford toured
twenty-nine countries making a joyful noise unto the
Lord. He recently won an Obie Award as the best actor in
a musical for his performance in *Don't Bother Me, I Can't
Cope.* His recording of his own song, "Too Close to
Heaven," has sold over two and a half million copies. He
and his various groups can be heard on such recording
labels as Atlantic and Columbia and on major television
shows in the U.S.A., Canada, England, and elsewhere. An
ordained minister, Bradford has long been associated with
Abyssinian Baptist Church in Newark. In this conversation, Bradford discusses his own career, the history and
the future of gospel music.

ABDUL: Although much of the music of today's youth
has borrowed heavily from gospel music, very little is
known of its origins. When did gospel music come into
being?

BRADFORD: Not only have they borrowed heavily, they

have *mutilated* gospel music. They have tried to kill our music, but they haven't succeeded, because it lives on. It's a music that brings peace to people, it's a music that unites people, and that's why gospel music will live on, because of the dedication and real interest behind it. The father of gospel music is Dr. Thomas A. Dorsey. Dr. Dorsey was once known as Georgia Tom and he was the pianist for Bessie Smith, Mamie Smith, and Trixie Smith.

ABDUL: These were famous blues singers.

BRADFORD: Yes. During this time in his personal life, a very serious thing happened. His wife died in childbirth and he couldn't get back home because he had to work. It was at this time that he decided to give *God* his heart, and it was from this experience that he wrote his famous song "Precious Lord, Take My Hand."

ABDUL: In other words, "Precious Lord" is one of the first gospel songs?

BRADFORD: That's right. It was born out of suffering. And that is what gospel is. It is born out of the suffering of a people. All of the songs are not about suffering, however. Some are about our joys, the high points of our lives. Now, here is where the blues come in. Dr. Dorsey was a blues pianist. When he came into the religious field, he brought the beat and harmonies of the blues, the fields, the clubs, theatres, into the church. He mixed that with the spirituals and the field songs and the reels he had heard all his life. So, one is the big sister to the other. And Thomas A. Dorsey, who has never been a singer, recruited one of the best singers he could find—Sally Martin. So, she is rightfully the *mother* of gospel music. They went from church to church around the country where he would play and she would sing. Finally, they published one ten-cent sheet of music called "If You See My Savior."

ABDUL: And they finally settled down in Chicago?

BRADFORD: Yes. And Dr. Dorsey organized the first gospel choir in Chicago. From the choir, they went all over the country setting up gospel groups, and from that nucleus has emerged the National Convention of Gospel Choirs—now in its fortieth year. I am president of the New Jersey chapter.

ABDUL: There are many purists who believe that gospel music should only be performed in the church. Since you have had a career in the theatre, I'm curious about how you feel about this.

BRADFORD: I do not believe that gospel music belongs solely in the church. I know that it comes from the church—it had its beginnings in the church—but it belongs to the people. Gospel music is just like the gospel of Jesus. It has to be taken to the people. Jesus said: "Go, ye, to *all* the world." And if you are going to be a gospel singer, you have to take the message of Jesus to the people.

ABDUL: How did you happen to go into gospel music?

BRADFORD: I was in boarding school at Snow Hill Institute. I went home one weekend, and the Roberta Martin Singers and the Clara Ward Singers were appearing in Birmingham. The concert took place at Legion Field, and almost twenty thousand people came from as far as a hundred and fifty miles away. People brought their own chairs on top of their cars so that they could sit down and hear these wonderful people. And Roberta Martin sang "He Knows How Much I Can Bear." That was the song that turned me away from Wagner, Tchaikovsky, and

Chopin. That song was the most burning testimony I had ever heard. And I went back to school on Monday, and during the choir rehearsal, I taught the school choir that song. Mr. Brooks, our music teacher, didn't know it. On Sunday morning in Sunday School, he was late getting there, and it was my job to start. And when he walked in, the choir was singing "How Much I Can Bear." This had never been done at that school before. We usually sang only Methodist hymns. When he heard this, he physically assaulted me. I was afraid to tell my mother, because she would have punished me further. Anyway, I arranged with a friend of mine to send a telegram that I had to come home at once, and that's how I left school. Mr. Brooks berated me: "Gospel music is *trash*. You'll never get anywhere with that. Nobody wants to hear it. And you could be a sensational musician. You are not going to get anywhere." Exactly six weeks after I left school, I signed my first broadcasting contract!

ABDUL: How did that happen?

BRADFORD: My mother was an insurance agent, and the company had a broadcast four times a week. They had a group which was singing spirituals and it was getting nowhere with the public. So, when I came along, I taught the group some gospel songs, and immediately our audience multiplied. Several months after I left school, I was making a hundred dollars a week, which was more than my school teacher made a month. Later that year, I went on tour with my group from Alabama.

ABDUL: This was the group which appeared on the broadcasts.

BRADFORD: Yes. The name of the insurance company

which sponsored us was called Protective Industrial so the group was called The Protective Harmoneers. We went to Detroit because my sister had a group there, and they invited us to appear for their anniversary. We were such a hit that another group from Detroit called the Birdettes asked me to appear with them. To make a long story short, the Birdettes hired me. The Protective Harmoneers were all married people, and they had to go back home. So I stayed with the Birdettes until Miss Bird dismissed us for some reason. In that group were the Banks family and they took me on to Pittsburgh with them. And there we met Elder Beck and others. I stayed until my brother in New York sent for me.

ABDUL: How did you come to New York?

BRADFORD: By bus. I took a job at Horn and Hardart and I still have the card. I can go back to Horn and Hardart whenever I wish. From Horn and Hardart, I started working for the Brandt Theatre chain on Forty-second Street. And that is what I wanted. I went from theatre to theatre and this was my school.

ABDUL: This gave you a chance to see all of those good movies.

BRADFORD: I studied actresses like Elizabeth Bergner, Bette Davis, and Joan Crawford, and the actors Edward G. Robinson and Van Heflin. I went every day and studied their moods. During that time, I had my first group in the Bronx called the Gospelaires and I also tutored a couple of quartets. Then the Ward Singers brought me to the Golden Gate Auditorium.

ABDUL: How did they find out about you?

BRADFORD: Because I had the Bronx Gospelaires.

Johnny Miles was the great promoter then and he introduced us as a new group which had won some kind of contest. I went back to Alabama—because I had to go back to school—and I started playing for the church choir. But every summer I would come back, and Langston Hughes, the great man that he was, saw me and catalogued me in his mind. Eventually, in 1953 I came out with my big hit record, "Too Close to Heaven."

ABDUL: What kind of record sales did you have from this record?

BRADFORD: Phenomenal. They never expected it. I was writing my own stuff. By this time I had worked with Sally Martin, Dr. Dorsey, Mahalia Jackson, Clara Ward, and a little bit of them had rubbed off on me. Fred Barr and Doc Wheeler saw me and decided to take the first gospel show into the Apollo Theatre.

ABDUL: Who was featured on that bill?

BRADFORD: It was Alex Bradford, the Pilgrim Travellers, the Soul Stirrers, Brother Joe May, Ethel Davenport, Clara Ward, and others.

ABDUL: What was the audience response to a bill like that?

BRADFORD: They had lines around three blocks.

ABDUL: And from the Apollo, where did you go?

BRADFORD: We went to Madison Square Garden, Carnegie Hall, and Town Hall. Then Langston was ready. He wrote *Black Nativity* for Marian Williams, Princess Stewart, and myself. It opened at the Forty-first Street Theatre and ran about seven months. Then we went to Spoleto [Italy] and on to twenty-nine countries for the next four years.

ABDUL: When you returned to the United States, did

you find it difficult to reestablish yourself in gospel circles?

BRADFORD: Fortunately, I had my own church, where I am now—Greater Abyssinian. My work went on during my absence, because I had my assistants there. When I came back, I had a place to go. But, there was a lean period because, while I was gone, the record world was making other groups.

ABDUL: What was your first "big" thing after your return to the United States?

BRADFORD: The *Love Festival* in Newark, produced by Tony Lawrence. Nobody thought Newark could do it. But they produced it there, and it drew over 110,000 people. Then I was signed by Atlantic Records and I did another show with Vinnette Carroll called *Bury the Dead*. We revived *Black Nativity* for the Christmas season, then she and Micki Grant collaborated on *Don't Bother Me, I Can't Cope*.

ABDUL: Which brought you back to Broadway.

BRADFORD: In the fullest sense. For this play I won the Obie Award as the best actor in a musical.

ABDUL: What are your plans for the future?

BRADFORD: Well, I've written my own production, *Black Seeds of Music,* which my group performs in the educational network.

ABDUL: In this way, you are spreading the gospel to young people.

BRADFORD: Yes, because we really need more young people to take on the faith. Gospel music will never die as long as we have them.

ABDUL: Who do you think will be the stars of the future on the gospel scene?

BRADFORD: Well, I certainly think that Bobby Hill, who

is also in *Cope,* will be one of the greatest. Not only does he sing, but he plays piano, teaches choirs, and writes. There is a great young writer out in California, Isaiah Jones, who used to work with me. And there is Cassetta George, who used to be a member of the Caravans, and Inez Andrews from Birmingham, who really moves mountains.

ABDUL: And what about Chicago, which for so long was the center of gospel music?

BRADFORD: Jessie Dickson heads them all out there as a writer, a musician, and singer. Then there is a young woman with several hit records by the name of Maggie Bell.

ABDUL: Do you feel that gospel music will be able to survive the great amount of exposure it is getting through the current popular music forms?

BRADFORD: It's going to last because it involves many people of all ages. I predict that it is going to outlast this new stuff they are trying to do. It will live and stand by the rest of the music because it is a native art form that belongs to black Americans.

JAMES DePRIEST
Symphonic Conductor

𝒫HILADELPHIA-BORN James DePriest is associate conductor of the National Symphony (Washington, D.C.), one of the handful of blacks to hold such a position. A first-prize winner of the Mitropoulos International Conductors Competition, he was assistant conductor of the New York Philharmonic for a season, after which he appeared as guest conductor with such important European orchestras as those of Rotterdam, Stockholm, Brussels, and Berlin. In the United States he has been guest conductor of major orchestras including those of New York, Philadelphia, Chicago, Pittsburgh, Minnesota, Cleveland, Boston, Los Angeles, as well as the interracial Symphony of the New World (New York). The following excerpts from a conversation in his New York apartment take the reader into the fascinating world of an outstanding young American conductor.

ABDUL: Did the fact that your aunt, Marian Anderson, was one of the world's most famous singers have any bearing on your choice to make a career in music?

DePRIEST: Well, I lived in a very musical home. I studied piano like most young people did at that time. My mother was also a fine singer and there were always recordings in the home. There was a tradition of listening to opera and to concert broadcasts, but I don't recall any special impact that music made upon me.

ABDUL: So nobody tried to force music on you?

DEPRIEST: No. The result of that "nonforcing" was that when I went into the University of Pennsylvania, I worked toward a B.S. in economics because I planned to be a lawyer. I hadn't the slightest idea of pursuing music as a career. I remember that when I was in high school, however, Dr. Lewis Werson got many of us who eventually went into music "hooked" because of his enthusiasm. I played timpany and percussion in the all-Philadelphia Senior High School Orchestra. If there was any planting of a seed, performingwise, it was in the course of being in the orchestras in Philadelphia schools.

ABDUL: Did you continue your musical pursuits at college?

DEPRIEST: While I was at Penn, I was taking electives in the music department. And I was also actively involved with jazz, presenting a series of concerts which involved both jazz and nonjazz elements and lighting—it was a mixed-media thing—but still this was an avocation. After I was graduated from Penn, I was commissioned to write a ballet score for the Philadelphia Dance Company, which I accepted. By 1959, I decided that I would go to the Philadelphia Conservatory and take some select courses in harmony and orchestration and study composition with Vincent Persichetti. Still, I was so undecided about entering music that I went on to graduate school and got a master's degree in communications. Then the State Department asked me if I would be interested in doing a tour as an

American specialist in the Far and Near East in 1962.

ABDUL: Did you accept that offer?

DEPRIEST: I accepted the tour and the first stop was Bangkok. Ostensibly, the purpose there was to work with the jazz musicians due to the influence of the King, who was an amateur jazz saxophonist and clarinet player. By accident, I found there was a symphony orchestra connected with the Ministry of Culture. I asked a friend of mine to take me to a rehearsal. They were rehearsing the Schubert C Major Symphony and they asked me if I would rehearse with them. I had never, of course, conducted that symphony, but it was one of several albums my aunt had given me as a teen-ager and to which I had listened. The musicians responded to what I was doing. Everything felt so natural about the music. I discovered at that point that *that* was what I wanted to do.

ABDUL: When you made this decision, did you ever stop to think that the possibilities were very limited for a black conductor?

DEPRIEST: From junior high school forward, I never thought anything about being inhibited from doing anything I wanted to do. A major problem at that time was to find out how significant the ability was. In ascertaining this, I continued on the tour to places where the orchestras were better and the same thing happened—the musicians responded.

ABDUL: Wasn't it in Thailand that you came down with polio?

DEPRIEST: One morning when I got up, I couldn't put any pressure on the bottom of my right foot and I came down with a fever. I went to the doctor and he gave me something to bring down the fever and told me to go to

46

bed. The next morning I couldn't stand up, so I called the embassy and they sent over a doctor and I went to the hospital for tests. He came back and said: "I have bad news for you. You have polio."

[DePriest was flown back to Philadelphia, where he began his long road to recovery. Besides learning to walk again, he plunged himself into preparations for the 1963 Mitropoulos International Conductors Competition, which he was determined to enter.]

DEPRIEST: I was rather apprehensive about what was going to happen when I went to New York for the competition because I thought that they would have all the hotshot young American conductors who had been in Europe. So I went in and I conducted the first movement of the Tchaikovsky *Pathetique*. This was my first opportunity before a professional American orchestra doing music of the standard repertoire. Needless to say, I had never conducted any of these things before. It was exactly the same as it had been before every place else in the course of the tour, except that the sound was glorious and I *knew* that I could do it. So, of the hundred American conductors to which they listened, there were seven who were picked to represent the United States and I was one of the seven. By the time we reached the semifinals, there were only two Americans left and neither of us went beyond that.

[In 1964, DePriest entered the competition again and emerged as a first-prize winner. After a season as an assistant conductor of the New York Philharmonic

(1965–66), he found himself with no prospects for the future. He and his wife moved to Rotterdam (Holland), where his friend Edo De Waart was conductor of the orchestra.]

DePriest: In December of 1967, my friend Edo De Waart called me and told me that he had to be in London during the 1968–69 season and he could not do four of his concerts in Rotterdam scheduled for February. He asked the management to let me do them. That was to be my European debut. It is very rare at that point in careers that conductors help each other.

Abdul: I know. It is a question of self-preservation.

DePriest: Literally everything was hinging on the success of that debut concert in Rotterdam. Not a modest success or good results, but everything had to be absolutely sensational.

Abdul: You must have felt like a circus performer.

DePriest: In a way I did. I said, "This is really insane. I have to eat and survive and it's dependent upon how well a lot of people I've never met respond to me on the platform and how people write about me in the newspaper."

Abdul: Was the concert a success?

DePriest: It was everything I could hope for, plus some. *Everything* followed. The next concerts I did were in Stockholm. Rotterdam reengaged me for five or six concerts. I went to Stockholm and *that* success was even greater than Rotterdam. Two weeks later Kubelik got ill and I went back to Stockholm to replace him and work with André Watts for the first time. And that cemented my success in Stockholm and resulted in my re-

turning every year for longer periods. I went on to
Belgium, Germany, and Italy. Then, a letter came from
the Hurok office—"Dear Jimmy." [Sol Hurok, who had
managed his famous aunt's career, was prepared to take
over his.]

[On both sides of the Atlantic, more and more engagements followed. One of the most memorable,
however, was the opportunity to conduct the National
Symphony of Washington, D.C., in Constitution Hall
where, many years ago, his aunt, Marian Anderson,
was refused the right to sing.]

DePRIEST: Antol Dorati asked me to come to Washington to conduct the National Symphony in 1970 when they
were still in Constitution Hall. That was a very emotional
moment because that is the same hall where my aunt could
not appear. But, it was so *simple* for me. I just went in and
walked out on the stage. That was a very special moment.
ABDUL: Was she present at the concert?
DePRIEST: No. But I called her the night after the first
rehearsal and told her how I felt.

[Not long after that appearance, DePriest was
engaged by the National Symphony as its associate
conductor, making him one of the few blacks holding
such a position.]

ABDUL: When you are confronted with the question of
the relevance of European symphonic music to blacks,
how do you handle it?

49

DePriest: Music, whether or not it happens to be Western European, is for human beings. It can be enlightening,
enriching. It can be a meaningful encounter regardless of
racial, ethnic, or national orientation. But for blacks in
America, there is nothing that is alien in classical music in
terms of its essence. What one wants to get in the soul of
Beethoven is as easily perceived and is as relevant to a
black human being as to a white human being, because the
soul of Beethoven, the *soul* of Mozart, the *soul* of Brahms or
any composer of *any* music speaks directly to the human
heart. It penetrates through all the layers of superficiality,
of all the layers of accumulated doctrine, all of the layers
of acculturation—it gets to you in essence where you *are*
just like everyone else. The first experience is the human
experience which transcends race, so that pain, happiness,
depression, exultation—all of the basic human emotions
that have nothing to do with race—are affected by music.
The black experience is on top of this, which gives a special
character. If I find something that is elevating or that
elates me, the way which I will vocally manifest that will be
entirely different from a white person's expression. The
way I will show *my* grief or anger will be *different,* but the
anger and the grief and the exultation are fundamental
human emotions and these are the emotions that I try to
touch—have the music touch—and convey *that* to audiences. And, in that sense, classical music is relevant to anyone who wants to give himself over to it.

GLORIA FOSTER
Actress

"Most moving of all is Gloria Foster, a young actress with talent and intensity to burn. Three of her turns are in themselves justification for a visit to *In White America*. As a Negro woman who had thirteen children, all sold into slavery, but who never lost her zest for life, she delivers a speech defending women's rights with rich earthy gusto.

"She is ravaged by tightlipped furies as a woman telling of her husband's lynching and her own abuse by the Ku Klux Klan. And she is heartbreaking as the girl who first attempted to integrate Central High in Little Rock, Arkansas. Someone should write a play for Miss Foster, and it could be one with music, for she has a full, deep singing voice."

Howard Taubman
The New York Times
November 1, 1963

"Fireworks are exploding every night over Herald Square—or, to be more precise, in a large, first-floor room at the Hotel Martinique.

"The best version in English of Euripides' 2,400-year-old tale of vengeance, Robinson Jeffers' ever-fresh, majestic *Medea*, is blazing at this midtown hotel. *Medea* springs to passionate stage life because of the soaring performance of Gloria Foster in the title role. Miss Foster, a comparative newcomer to New York theatre, garnered praise two seasons ago with several powerful vignettes in Martin Duber-

51

man's distinguished *In White America*. A lovely young black actress, with a voluptuous figure and hauntingly expressive eyes, Miss Foster now proves definitively that she is one of the most exciting talents in the American theatre. She performs Medea with the outsized gestures of a Graham dancer or an actress in opera. Yet she always sees to it that her Medea is a recognizable woman, a lady committed to the rage of love. She clearly understands the musicality of the work, sensing when to diminish a note and when to play fortissimo. Many critics pointed out that on opening night, she played in one key throughout. Perhaps. I caught her performance on the fourth night, and it was a model of variety and nuance. Miss Foster provides one of the few genuinely enchanted evenings this season. One can only weep at the beauty of her portrayal.

"The rest of the production? So-so . . . ho-hum. Helen Craig is impressive as the Nurse, and Michael Higgins rather effective as Jason. But some of the performers in minor roles are embarrassingly bad. The setting by David Mitchell, a handsome assemblage of stones to form the doorway of Medea's house, is very, very good. But the electricity, more powerful than anything Con Ed has to offer, is supplied by a great artist, Miss Gloria Foster."

Emory Lewis
Cue
December 11, 1965

"Gloria Foster's Madame Ranevskaya had the right wan and disillusioned confidence of a woman, brought up in riches, dangerously uncaring for the future."

Clive Barnes
The New York Times
January 12, 1973

ACCLAIMED BY critics as one of the finest young dramatic actresses on the American stage, Gloria Foster burst on the New York scene with her electric performance in *In White America,* for which she received the Vernon Rice Award and the first Obie for the best performance in an off-Broadway show. Subsequently, she won the Theatre World Award and a second Obie for her portrayal of *Medea,* after which she was highly acclaimed for her work in *Yerma, Sister Sonji,* and *The Cherry Orchard.* Her screen appearances have included *Nothing But a Man, The Comedians,* and *Man and Boy.* On television she costarred with Bill Cosby in the CBS Emmy award-winning "To All My Friends on Shore." Offstage, she is the wife of actor Clarence Williams III. The following conversation took place backstage at the New York Shakespeare Festival Public Theater, where she was playing the leading role in an all-black production of *The Cherry Orchard.*

ABDUL: What would you consider your first major appearance in New York?

FOSTER: Well, my first professional experience here in New York was in 1963. That was in *In White America.* That was my maiden voyage off-Broadway.

ABDUL: Have you made any movies?

FOSTER: Very few and they have not necessarily been starring roles. I am very proud to have been a part of the film *Nothing But a Man,* which was among the first I made. I had done *The Cool World* with Shirley Clark, which came along when that sort of film was not being made. Then I did *The Comedians.* And I've done *Man and Boy* with Bill

Cosby. I think that it was a lovely, sensitive, warm story about a man and his son in a Western environment.

ABDUL: And you did a very impressive television film about sickle-cell anemia.

FOSTER: It was one of those rare opportunities to do something informative as well as entertaining. I've been fortunate enough to have the opportunity to make a social comment as well as a dramatic statement such as *In White America*.

ABDUL: I've noticed that you've been very selective in choosing the roles which you've played.

FOSTER: I have to be selective. I came into this business to work, not just take a job. There are roles I have to play. There are emotions that I have to express. There are statements I would like to make. I have to find those characters in those plays that permit me to do my work.

ABDUL: There have been long periods of time between roles that you have played.

FOSTER: Yes. There were many months between jobs—months!

ABDUL: Because there are two actors in your household, is there any conflict when you are both working on roles at the same time?

FOSTER: No.

ABDUL: Where do you consider home—New York?

FOSTER: Home is where my husband is, but in terms of a physical setting, New York is our home.

ABDUL: When did you first realize that you wanted to become an actress or did you always know?

FOSTER: I knew I wanted some way of expressing myself on a public platform. When I was in college [Illinois State]

I participated in forensics as an extracurricular activity. I enjoyed competing in tournaments with other universities and found public response to my efforts very rewarding.

ABDUL: You mean that special thing that happens between audience and performer?

FOSTER: Right. I had gone to Illinois State with thoughts of becoming a teacher, but found that my honesty was not there. I wasn't interested in teaching. I was really interested in finding a platform on which I could affect people.

ABDUL: In all the articles I've read about you, I notice that you always give special credit to an instructor with whom you worked at the Goodman Memorial Theatre.

FOSTER: Yes. Dr. Bella Itkin. She taught me what I know about acting.

ABDUL: At this time, many people are divided on the question of whether black actors should be doing the classics or not. How do you feel about it?

FOSTER: I don't even deal with it. I've got work to do. I'm going to work at whatever I think I can do and I'm going to fail in some things and succeed in others, so I couldn't care less about what somebody says I'm supposed to do with my life. I was surprised that there was any kind of controversy over whether we should do a Chekhov play. Then, why read it in school? No, I have nothing to do with that.

ABDUL: What happens when you are actually studying a role? Do you just let the role "happen" to you?

FOSTER: No, I sometimes have to make it happen. It's pretty much reading a script to find out what similarities there are in the character and myself. Then, finding out what differences there are. And to find out *why* there are differences. Where that character is coming from, where she is going, then how she gets there. The "how" is why you rehearse. Many times I start drawing from experiences other people have had that I've been fortunate enough to witness. I start pulling out things from my emotional warehouse. Hopefully, when I get on my feet in a work situation with a director, he will lead me down the path to putting it all together.

ABDUL: Do you like working with a strong director?

FOSTER: I *have* to work with a strong director.

ABDUL: In view of the fact that you are articulate in expressing your attitudes toward the theatre, do you think that someday you might want to teach?

FOSTER: I've been asked to teach for a number of years. That's not where my honesty is. I want to act.

ABDUL: Did you enjoy working with James Earl Jones during the period he was actually directing *The Cherry Orchard*?

FOSTER: Yes. My specific reason for traveling three thousand miles, which is what I did, coming from California, was to develop Madame Ranevskaya under James Earl Jones. This was going to be his first experience as a director. I think that Madame Ranevskaya is perhaps the most difficult character I have ever played because there are very few similarities between that woman and myself. So, it was a great challenge, but I was prepared to fail or succeed under James Earl. The joy of it, the new experience of it, was going to be the possibility of being an instrument manipulated by a great actor in his first directorial situation.

ABDUL: What advice would you give a young person who wants to make a career in the theatre?

FOSTER: I would not advise them. They can read this interview. I could tell them of my own experiences. They could read about other actors' experiences. There is no one way or any sure way of becoming an actor.

ARETHA FRANKLIN
Queen of Soul

Aretha Franklin made her professional debut when she was twelve years old. She sang a solo in the church where her father was pastor. She was paid a fee of fifteen dollars and she immediately went out and bought a pair of roller skates.

Aretha was already a veteran performer, as she had started to sing in the church's youth choir when she was only eight. And it wasn't long afterward that she formed a gospel singing group with her older sister, Erma, and two other girls.

Meantime, she was trying to teach herself how to play the piano. At first it was more banging than playing, so her father engaged a piano teacher. But the teacher didn't teach the kind of music that interested Aretha. She remembers, "When she'd come, I'd hide." Fortunately, gospel singer and composer James Cleveland, who was a boarder in the Franklin home at the time, helped her. "He showed me some real nice chords," says Aretha.

Aretha Franklin was born in Memphis in 1942. Her father, the Reverend C. L. Franklin, is a nationally known revivalist preacher and gospel singer with many sermons on recordings. Aretha credits her father with being the major influence on her musical style. Her mother was also a gospel singer.

When Aretha was two years old, the family moved north, spending five years in Buffalo before settling permanently in Detroit. There, the Reverend Franklin became pastor of the New Bethel Baptist Church, which he built into one of the largest congregations in the Midwest, with 45,000 members.

Unlike Diana Ross, who grew up in the same neighborhood, Aretha was never poor and lived in a big house with a green lawn on a tree-shaded street. But it was not a happy home. Mrs. Franklin abandoned the family when Aretha was six and died a few years later. Reverend Franklin was often out of town on long preaching trips, sometimes a month at a time. Aretha and her two sisters and two brothers were left in the care of housekeepers. As the famous singer Mahalia Jackson said, "The whole family wanted for love." Aretha has never forgotten the loneliness of her childhood. The hurts she suffered then are reflected in the music she sings now.

But there were good times, too. The Franklin house was often filled with music, not only gospel music, but also blues and jazz, for the various branches of black music are related, having come from the same sources. Among those Aretha met while still very young, in addition to Mahalia Jackson and James Cleveland, were Clara Ward, Dinah Washington, Arthur Prysock, Lou Rawls, and B. B. King.

Aretha heard all of them sing. She listened and learned. Her favorite, perhaps, was gospel singer Clara Ward. When Aretha's aunt died, Miss Ward came to sing at the funeral. She sang "Peace in the Valley" and got so caught up in the music that she tore the hat from her head and flung it to the ground. That moment was when Aretha decided on a singing career.

At the age of fourteen, Aretha was already on her way. That year, she cut her first disks, gospel songs "Never Grow Old" and "Precious Lord, Take My Hand," recorded by a small company which sold exclusively in black communities.

About the same time and while she was a student at Detroit's Northern High School, Aretha began to travel with her father's gospel troupe. Reverend Franklin preached his fiery sermons and Aretha, backed by the choir, sang the exciting gospel songs. Many who heard her in those days predicted that she would become one of the great gospel singers.

But Aretha was not satisfied with her life as a member of her father's group. She did not like the constant travel, usually in a crowded car. She resented having to leave the main highways to find a place to eat or sleep, for at that time many restaurants and hotels were still closed to blacks.

One of the members of Reverend Franklin's choir, Sam Cooke, had left and gone on to great success as a pop singer. Aretha had known him well, and when she was eighteen, she decided to follow his example. She went to New York, found a manager and a vocal coach, and made some demonstration records.

One of the "demos," a song entitled "Today I Sing the Blues," was heard by John Hammond, the jazz impressario who was an executive of Columbia Records. Hammond, who discovered Billie Holiday and other greats, was very impressed. He said, "This is the best voice I've heard in twenty years." And he signed her to a recording contract.

During the next five years, Aretha made many singles and nine albums. She sang mostly standards, novelties, and jazz. Critics generally praised her, but none of the records became big hits. She appeared at the 1963 Newport Jazz Festival, toured Bermuda, the Bahamas, and Puerto Rico, but mostly she made the dreary round of rhythm and blues nightclubs along the "chitlin' circuit." She was sometimes so unhappy and even scared in these places that she often sang to the floor instead of to the audience.

The trouble was that she was not being herself. She was trying to be a glamorous pop singer, but the real Aretha had her roots in gospel and blues. That Aretha was not coming through. With her initial impact waning and her hopes of success fading, she did less and less singing and turned toward her home and family. She had married young and had three sons—Clarence, Edward, and Teddy. On Wednesday evenings she would go with her girlfriends from childhood to the roller rink. On Sunday evenings, she would return to her father's church and sing gospel solos.

But she had not abandoned her career—she was only waiting for a chance to make a new beginning. She was too young to give up, though sometimes she did not feel so young. "Twenty-five going on sixty-five," as she put it. When the Columbia Records contract finally ran out, she was offered a new one, which she refused, and signed instead with Atlantic. In the more sympathetic atmosphere of this firm, which specialized in "soul," she could have maximum freedom as a performer. She could choose her songs and she could sing them the way she wanted. She could be herself.

Her first Atlantic single, "I Never Loved a Man (the Way I Love You)," was released in February 1967. That was the start of her amazing second career. Suddenly everything went right. The new Aretha made one hit record after another. That first year she had five certified Gold Records. (Gold Records are awarded by the Recording Industry Association for every single that sells a million copies and every album that brings in a million dollars in wholesale receipts.)

In that incredible year of 1967, her personal appearances became triumphs. She stole the show at the New York Jazz Festival on Randall's Island, brought a capacity audience at Philharmonic Hall to its feet cheering. She appeared with Johnny Carson on "The Tonight Show." She made a seven-city tour with Harry Belafonte for the benefit of the Reverend Martin Luther King, Jr.'s Southern Christian Leadership Conference and received a citation from that organization. *Time* did a five-page feature on her. The leading show business magazines, *Billboard*, *Cashbox*, and *Record World* chose her as Female Vocalist of the Year.

Unlike so many popular performers, Aretha was not a one-year wonder. She has continued to pour out a steady stream of hit records which have won her many more Gold Records and numerous Grammy Awards for best-record performances. She has had her own TV special and appeared on all the major TV interview and variety programs. She sang "The Star Spangled Banner" at the 1968 Democratic National Convention—a "soul" version. She has toured Europe and sung in nightclubs, halls, arenas, and stadiums in every corner of America.

Aretha on stage in concert is a wild torrent of energy, zest, and strength. She is anything but the shy and withdrawn person interviewers often find her. A friend has remarked that "Aretha comes alive only when she's singing," and certainly the performance she gives pulsates with life. Indeed, it is more than a performance—it is an experience, exciting and electrifying. She moves toward the edge of the stage to get closer to the audience. "If they don't happen, I don't happen," she admits. But when it does happen, with the audience joining in, responding with shouts and rhythmic clapping, it seems like an old-fashioned Baptist revival meeting. Thus Aretha re-creates for people of all races and religions the atmosphere in which she grew up.

What transformed Aretha from just another popular singer who wasn't making any advance into becoming a superstar or, indeed, a national institution? The answer begins with the material, the songs she sings. She chooses them very carefully—she has learned the hard way not to let other people tell her what to sing. She explains it this way: "If a song's about something I've experienced or that could've happened to me, it's good. But if it's alien to me, I couldn't lend anything to it."

One way to make sure a song is right for her is to write it herself. The fact that she composes many of her own songs is not widely known, because her fame as a singer has overshadowed her ability as a composer. Though she hardly reads a note of music, she blocks out arrangements for most of the songs she performs. She frequently accompanies herself on the piano both in records and concerts. She has even been known to be a part of her own background chorus through a process known as overdubbing. Thus, by reason of her multiple talents as a musician, an Aretha Franklin song—whether it was written by her or someone else—emerges as a total concept with an unusual consistency of style and content.

"I sing to people about what matters," Aretha says. "I express problems." Most are problems all of us have, such as growing up. As she puts it, "Trying to grow up is hurting. You make mistakes. You try to learn from them, and when you don't, it hurts even more. And I've been hurt—hurt bad." She has an uncanny ability to express the basic human emotions in her singing. "It seems simple to me," she says, "but for some people, I guess, feelin' takes courage."

Instead of trying to be everything to everybody, she digs deep inside herself. There she finds the loneliness of a little child who has lost her mother, the fear of being on your own in a big world, the exultation that sometimes comes in church, the joy when somebody loves you, and the heartache when somebody doesn't.

Aretha has, of course, reaped the material rewards of her success. For a number of years, she lived in a big, comfortable house in Detroit—she now lives in New York City. Friends report, however, that she isn't always happy. Maybe that is why the hurt still comes through when she sings. "It's hard to laugh when you want to cry," she says. "Some people can hide it. I can't, so when I sing, it doesn't come across fake."

And that's the real secret of the success of her second career. Call it honesty or sincerity or being yourself. Or call it *soul*. There is the quality of genuineness about Aretha's work that cannot be put on. So, they call her "Queen of Soul" or simply "Lady Soul," which is the title of one of her albums.

Her music is black music, grown out of the black experience in America. All American popular music has its roots in black culture, but until recent times, it has been diluted and distorted to suit the tastes of a white audience. Aretha sings it like it is. Immersed from early childhood in gospel and blues, she sings the real thing, black and beautiful. And she has come along at a time when almost everybody, regardless of color, is ready to listen. For, as Aretha says, "You don't have to be Negro to have soul. It's not cool to be Negro or Jewish or Italian or anything else. It's just cool to be alive, to be around."

That's about as close to a speech as Aretha has come. But one of her first big records, "Respect," came to symbolize the movement for black equality. R-E-S-P-E-C-T. "If you've got that," says Aretha, "you can get the rest of it. Without it, you can't put anything together."

MICKI GRANT
Composer - Lyricist and Performer

Cʜɪᴄᴀɢᴏ-ʙᴏʀɴ Micki Grant recently burst on the Broadway scene as the composer-lyricist of the long-running musical *Don't Bother Me, I Can't Cope,* which was showered with many honors, including the 1972 Grammy Award as "Best Broadway Musical Cast Album of the Year." Before long, other successful productions of the show, which was conceived and directed by Vinnette Carroll, opened in Chicago, Los Angeles, and Toronto. Cast either as actress or singer (or sometimes both), Micki Grant has been highly praised in such shows as *Tambourines to Glory, Brecht on Brecht, Leonard Bernstein's Theatre Songs, The Cradle Will Rock, The Blacks, Jericho-Jim Crow* and *To Be Young, Gifted and Black.* She has also appeared as Peggy Nolan on the daytime television serial "Another World." In this conversation, which took place in her dressing room at the Edison Theatre in New York, she discusses her work as composer-lyricist, actress, singer, and her hopes for the future of black people in the theatre.

Aʙᴅᴜʟ: When you wrote *Don't Bother Me, I Can't Cope,* did you ever stop and think that the role of composer-lyricist of the musical theatre was an unusual one for a woman?

GRANT: No, not until afterward when people started pointing it out to me.

ABDUL: When did you start writing songs and lyrics?

GRANT: When I was a teen-ager. I started writing poetry before I wrote music—around the age of eight.

ABDUL: What kind of musical training did you have?

GRANT: I started studying violin at nine, so by the time I started writing songs, I had some musical background. After the violin, I went on to study the double bass and I took the mandatory amount of theory and harmony.

ABDUL: When you compose, do you sit down and write down your ideas directly on paper or do you have to hear the notes on the piano?

GRANT: I use a piano to write my melody line. Then I usually work out my chords on a guitar.

ABDUL: Do you give it to somebody else to arrange and orchestrate?

GRANT: I never do the arrangements. I give it to an arranger, but the arranger and I usually work together because I *hear* what I want.

ABDUL: When did you first get the idea to put your songs together into a larger format—a musical?

GRANT: To be honest with you, it wasn't my idea. It was Vinnette Carroll's idea.

ABDUL: How did she happen to think of you?

GRANT: She was looking for someone to do a musical version of *Bury the Dead.* She auditioned several people, but she hadn't heard anyone who she felt was right. Glory Van Scott showed her some things I had written and she invited me to come down to the Urban Theatre Corps and play a few things. She said that this was the sound she had been looking for, so we started working. Ironically, *Cope* came first even though it wasn't planned that way. She wanted to present a piece at the Library for the Performing Arts and she wanted to utilize my material for it. We began to work, and it became bigger and bigger. She called in gospel singers, dancers, and a choreographer. I was supposed to do the songs and then go on my vacation, but I couldn't tear myself away from the rehearsals. A few days before the first preview, Vinnette decided that I was to perform in the show.

ABDUL: So, this project, which really started out for the Library of the Performing Arts, eventually became *Don't Bother Me, I Can't Cope*?

GRANT: It always was the title. It got such tremendous response—I don't think I was prepared for that kind of response—and suddenly publishers and personal managers started coming around and showing interest. It took about a year before we got commercially launched because we did a special performance for the directors of the Ford Theatre [Washington, D.C.] and they decided they wanted to open their season with it.

ABDUL: I've seen the production in its different forms. I saw it in Washington at the Ford, which is basically the way it was performed in New York. Then again, I saw it in California where they wrote out your role and divided your songs among the entire cast. Were you in a state of shock when you saw all of those changes on the Coast?

GRANT: No, I thought it was beautiful. The concept for the show is Vinnette's anyway—all the staging and what have you—originated right out of her head. The reason I

68

was blocked in the New York version the way I was is because I am the author. Vinnette says that there would be no validity in staging anyone else the same way. It's kind of marvelous to see how the material works in so many forms, and *that* pleases me. It makes me feel there is something in the material. When I saw the reaction of the audience in Los Angeles, I was just delighted.

ABDUL: Who took your part in the New York company when you flew out to California to see the show?

GRANT: Vivian Reed took my part, and when they opened the Chicago company, she went out there to do it.

ABDUL: Is the Chicago production similar to New York?

GRANT: No, it's very similar to the Coast. In fact, all productions from here on in will be done that way.

ABDUL: Have your folks seen the show?

GRANT: That is really a marvelous story. You see, I have a very large family and every two years we have a reunion somewhere. It just happened that we had planned to meet in Los Angeles in 1972. Nobody had any idea that *Cope* would be playing there at that time. And at the time of the opening, there we were—about fifty or sixty people from the same family.

ABDUL: Have you started something new?

GRANT: Yes, we finally did *Step Lively,* which is what we initially got together to do. It is being paired with *Croesus and the Witch* and is being done at the Urban Arts Corps with great success.

ABDUL: What are you going to be doing in the future? You are an actress and singer as well as songwriter-lyricist—how do you divide the many parts of your personality? Does that present any problems?

GRANT: I am hoping that it won't. But I find that this new area is really exciting. I love acting and singing, but in this way you get a chance to express your *own* ideas.

ABDUL: When did you start out in the theatre?

GRANT: I was about eight years old and I played the Spirit of Spring in a community center production in Chicago. Later, I joined a community group at the Wabash "Y" called the Center Aisle Players.

ABDUL: Was this an all-black group?

GRANT: Yes. Everybody volunteered their services—we all had other jobs—it was something we did out of love. But I was really serious about it and I think some of them thought I was being a little foolish when I said I was considering making a career as an actress.

ABDUL: Were your early visions of being in things like *Gone with the Wind* and being like Butterfly McQueen or did you simply assume that you could be a leading lady without regard to the type-casting of that time?

GRANT: I never identified with the black images that had been shown me on the screen. They were always being made fun of and put in laughable situations or they were running scared. That wasn't the image I had of myself. When you think of all of those people—if they had been given other parts—they were obviously very talented actors. But our images were being drawn for us by The Man.

ABDUL: To some extent they are still being drawn by other people. Even our own playwrights have, for the longest time, created the kind of black images that *white* critics told them to create. You knew that white audiences wouldn't accept certain things, so you wrote plays to fit the formula. They were black plays in a way, but they were really *white* black plays.

GRANT: I think that is the exciting thing that's happening now. Blacks are going away from the formula and depicting their own images the way *they* see them. And sometimes it is not always the images we would like, which actually shows the variations of viewpoint—all blacks are not alike.

ABDUL: Yes, but unfortunately we are top-heavy with another type of image in the theatre and that is Super Spade and Super Spade Chick.

GRANT: I think it's all going to balance out. You go from one extreme to another until you settle down to a norm.

ABDUL: What kind of advice would you give a young person who felt he might like to become a composer-lyricist in the theatre?

GRANT: I would see as much theatre as possible. And I would devote a whole lot of time to the study of musical theory and harmony, because I find that it is more important to have a knowledge of the workings of music rather than mastery of an instrument. I know many people who are writing today with no background in music—they hear marvelous melodies in their heads—but, if you are depending on someone else to write them down for you, there's no way for you really to check it out. You've got to be able to have control over what you are creating.

ABDUL: Do you think that if a black person really prepared himself in this field there would be opportunities for him in the musical theatre?

GRANT: I think that it is opening up more and more, and I also think that we should have some control at the top.

ABDUL: You mean like becoming producers?

GRANT: Yes. Because more and more talent is finding its way into the theatre because there are more opportunities today than there were, say, twenty years ago.

ABDUL: By the way, back in the twenties there was a whole decade of black-written and -produced musicals on Broadway and they disappeared from the scene never to come back.

GRANT: I know.

ABDUL: If you read accounts in the newspapers of their day, these shows were up to the highest standards of their time.

GRANT: Some of the songs that came out of them are still being sung today.

ABDUL: It seems most unusual that this great flowering of black talent did not culminate into something more lasting.

GRANT: I hope that we will get to the point where a fine composer or lyricist, although he is black, is not expected just to do black theatre. I hope that if a producer is about to do a half-million-dollar production and is looking for a composer or lyricist—and the best one happens to be black—I hope he will hire him.

ELLIS HAIZLIP
Television Producer

AFTER ITS FIRST year on New York's educational station, Channel 13, the Harris poll revealed that "Soul!" was watched every week by over half of the black viewers in the metropolitan area. Since that time, "Soul!" has become nationally syndicated and shown throughout the country. The executive producer of "Soul!" is Ellis Haizlip, who began his career in Washington, D.C., where he produced the Howard Players in their summer season at Howard University. After moving to New York, Haizlip became associated with Vinnette Carroll in productions at the Harlem YMCA and in the world tour of Langston Hughes's gospel song-play *Black Nativity*. With his own production company, he organized international tours of the Donald McKayle Dance Company's *Black New World*, James Baldwin's *The Amen Corner*, and Eugene O'Neill's *The Emperor Jones*. In this conversation, which took place in his office, Haizlip talks about the impact of "Soul!" on television programming in general as well as problems associated with keeping the program alive.

ABDUL: In what ways has "Soul!" had an impact on the television scene?

HAIZLIP: Well, the first thing you have to recognize is

73

that "Soul!" has had its greatest impact on educational television. Not so much on the programming aspect, but it brought to Channel 13, especially in its first year, a large increase in the black audience. One of the polls proved that more blacks were watching educational television than nonblacks. Subsequently, with the presentation of "Soul!" and "Black Journal" on educational television—and some other attitudinal programs like "Sesame Street," which although it is not a black show, is heavily promoted in the community—a lot of people got the impression that Channel 13 was indeed a station in which blacks had some control, which is not true. If the community had been sophisticated, perhaps they could have used the popularity of those programs to come in and seize some kind of control of programming, ideas, and attitudes by having a direct input into the administration of the station. When we first started, television consisted largely of variety shows and comedy shows on commercial channels. You had the very fast comedy shows like "Laugh-In" and "Love, American Style" and the situation comedies like those things that Danny Thomas did. But you very rarely saw the cultural experiences of young America being presented on television.

ABDUL: Television has always been backward in reflecting current life styles.

HAIZLIP: Except in the news. They are very much on top of things, but as far as culture is concerned . . . again, I don't think that the administration that was programming television was aware of the cultural changes taking place in the entire world. Blacks had reshaped definitions of music. Rhythm and Blues had finally made such a great impact.

ABDUL: Rhythm and Blues used to be kept in the closet, so to speak. Those recordings were sold almost exclusively in the black community.

HAIZLIP: As far as blacks are concerned, they are still in the closet. The whites have made the money from Rhythm and Blues—the Beatles imitating Little Richard, Joe Cocker using a gospel sound, Janis Joplin imitating other black performers. Eventually, "Soul!" had, I think, the influence of forcing programs like "In Concert" and "Midnight Special" to evolve. The audience is free to be able to express itself in relationship to a performance that it is enjoying as opposed to a performance that is being presented *for* it. And "Soul!" from its very inception was a "studio" show—an audience was there—and you were able to catch the flavor of people *interreacting*. Some sort of exchange was going on between performer and audience.

ABDUL: I've been recently watching reruns of "Soul!" and it's almost like being in the Apollo Theatre.

HAIZLIP: Or wherever. It's happening all over. I think "Soul!" is influential in giving those kinds of programs a start. This was a testing ground on public television.

ABDUL: What was the basic concept of "Soul!"?

HAIZLIP: To create a meaningful show that reflected the black experience which had not previously been shown on television. That meant dealing with a lot of Rhythm and Blues or classical black music. That's a quote of Rahsaan Roland Kirk. And the presentation of people in the literary field who had no exposure.

ABDUL: Could you tell me something about your own beginnings and what led up to your becoming a television producer?

HAIZLIP: I went to Howard University, and while I was there Owen Dodson, who was then in the drama department, gave me an opportunity to produce the Howard Players during the summer. That introduced me to theatrical production. And when I came to New York Vinnette Carroll gave me an opportunity to work with her at the Harlem YMCA.

ABDUL: That was when they presented *Dark of the Moon*. You had some marvelous people in that group.

HAIZLIP: *Dark of the Moon* was done there with Cicely Tyson, Clarence Williams III, Isabel Sanford, Calvin Lockhart, James Earl Jones, and the Alvin Ailey Dancers.

ABDUL: Weren't you involved in *Black Nativity* with Vinnette?

HAIZLIP: Yes, I was involved with *Black Nativity,* which was Langston Hughes's dream which really took gospel music around the world and did a lot to encourage the acceptance of gospel music as an art form. And then I started a production company of my own. I took the Donald McKayle Dance Company in a production called *Black New World* around the world and I took James Baldwin's *The Amen Corner* with Claudia McNeil on a world tour. Then I took James Earl Jones in *The Emperor Jones* on a European tour.

ABDUL: What did you do when you returned to the United States?

HAIZLIP: I was invited back after the uprisings in Watts and Newark to produce a television program that in some way would address itself to the black community. And, after many discussions, we came up with the idea of "Soul!" It was primarily *my* idea. It was quite a bit different from what the station had hoped to see. And the success of it is the thing that supported it, the reaction of the community to it, the reaction of the people who had to evaluate it. And, that's how "Soul!" started.

ABDUL: One of the things that has surprised me is the success you have had with poetry reading on "Soul!"

HAIZLIP: Well, the difference is that we've had the poets, people who look to their contributions to the culture of their people—they define themselves as poets as Bob Dylan defines himself as a songwriter and a performer of songs and his poetry is secondary. I suppose that "Soul!" has viewed poetry in much the same way as a part of black culture—the same way as the Russians view poetry as a part of Russian culture. I've been very turned on by poetry since our relationship with Langston Hughes, who viewed poetry as a folk idiom. It belongs to people in the same way as their dance and their music belongs to them. So, I've had no problem in dealing with a poet as though he were as valuable, as important, as entertaining (if that's the word you need to use), as enlightening, as enriching as a top performer. Leontyne Price, Aretha Franklin, and Imamu Baraka all stand on the same level to me as far as being able to deliver their message to the people and having it accepted.

ABDUL: How can a program with the large viewing public of "Soul!" run the risk of possibly being dropped from the airwaves?

HAIZLIP: Because "Soul!" was established at a time when the social climate dictated the *establishment* of such a program. At the moment, the climate dictates the *deprogramming* of such a program—and blacks are in *no* decision-making positions with regards to programming commercial or public television.

ABDUL: But blacks view television and they buy the products advertised on television.

HAIZLIP: That is irrelevant. It's the administration of this country that dictates . . . you're dealing with public television. There is a political board that controls public television.

ABDUL: In other words, whatever the political climate is currently reflects itself in what is on public television?

HAIZLIP: You find that the country is trying to move back to—they don't call it states' rights—but they're trying to deinvolve the federal government in the responsibility for its black citizens and place that responsibility again on a local level.

ABDUL: Well, there certainly has been a reaction to black progress. We are seeing retraction of many of the reforms made to insure further progress.

HAIZLIP: And the first thing you take away, of course, is the important communications media—which is television. So blacks are disappearing from television.

ABDUL: With the exception of a few commercial shows like "The Flip Wilson Show" and "Sanford and Son."

HAIZLIP: Flip Wilson does not *own* that network. The moment they wish to drop him, they *can* drop him. But, if the daughter of the man who owns the network has a show, then how easily can you drop her? So, politics is what rules the country, rules the programs—all programs—economic, social, spiritual—they are all controlled by the political fiber.

ABDUL: Well, you are certainly concerning yourself with

seeing that we are well represented on *educational* television.

HAIZLIP: This is because we are using government funds on Channel 13 and it behooves them to have black programming. Commercial television—you can boycott their products until they come around to reflecting your culture in the things that they sponsor.

ABDUL: Have you found that any of the large black organizations are interested in our plight in the field of television?

HAIZLIP: The Urban League, the National Council of Negro Women, and the Delta Sigma Theta Sorority have been responsive and have reacted positively to the things I needed in assisting my development and the growth of blacks in television.

ABDUL: What can the black community itself do to help change things?

HAIZLIP: I don't know what blacks can do except just recognize that they are *black,* then find the thing that is black they are most comfortable with, whether it is the local school board, church group, athletic club, or something you want to start. Now, if that in turn leads to electing officials, to gaining control of your local school board, if that in turn leads to your establishing a public health clinic—then we have to deal with it. But, the first thing to deal with is removing nonblacks from the decision-making processes that affect us.

JAMES EARL JONES
Actor

AT THE FINAL curtain of the Broadway premiere of *The Great White Hope* on October 3, 1968, the audience unanimously rose to its feet and gave its star, James Earl Jones, a standing ovation. In the days to follow, newspaper and magazine critics echoed this acclaim in some of the most glowing reviews accorded any black actor in recent times. The critic from *The New York Times* called him "a star—overnight," which reportedly amused Jones no end because he had been performing on the New York stage with great success since 1957, over a decade before he finally reached stardom.

In *The Great White Hope,* which won for its author, Howard Seckler, a Pulitzer Prize, he portrayed the role of a prizefighter based on the real-life first black heavyweight champion, Jack Johnson. Jack Kroll of *Newsweek* wrote, "The play is Jones—in him all the juggling and overdeliberation of the work become fused and ignited in a figure at once larger than life and densely human. Jones has a great big technique without the slightest trace of emptiness or inflation. He can expand before your eyes from a flare point of inarticulate feeling to a storm system of emotion." His outstanding performance was rewarded with the Tony Award as best dramatic actor in a Broadway play as well as

ALVIN AILEY

Kenn Duncan

MARTINA ARROYO

ALEX BRADFORD

JAMES DePRIEST

GLORIA FOSTER

ARETHA FRANKLIN

MICKI GRANT

ELLIS HAIZLIP

Bill Whiting, ENCORE *Magazine*

JAMES EARL JONES

ARTHUR MITCHELL

Martha Swope

RON O'NEAL

CARMAN MOORE

L. Bernikow

Diana Ross

Cicely Tyson

MELVIN VAN PEEBLES

Grace Harrington

BEN VEREEN

ANDRÉ WATTS

FLIP WILSON

the Drama Desk Award.

One evening, following a performance, Rex Reed asked Jones how he felt about his success in *The Great White Hope*. Did he feel humble, smug, or satisfied? Jones answered, "Well, none of those things, really. I often come home depressed because I know the audience stood and cheered but I want to be sure they do it for the right reasons. I want it to be for the play and for the company, not me. As for me, I rehearsed for six weeks in Washington, then played it seven weeks at the Arena Stage, and I'm only now beginning to see with a third eye where I belong. But I'm not there yet. I probably never will be. If you ever think that you've achieved perfection, it's the end of the road."

When he reported to work in Washington where the play was tried out, he plunged into the same kind of rigorous training that a fighter might in preparation for a championship fight. He read everything he could about Jack Johnson—books, clippings, articles—and studied the champion's old fight movies. It is said that his highly detailed notes on the role might lead a reader to believe that he was one of the most hostile people in the world. He had to draw from almost everything he had ever done previously on stage as well as from his own life experiences. It is said that he works in such detail because there is no score for an actor as there is for a singer. He said, "There's a script, but that's only a beginning."

Although Jones is highly articulate when it comes to discussing his work in the theatre, he is reluctant to talk about his personal life. When stopped on the street in his own neighborhood in the Chelsea section of New York, he is warm, friendly, and willing to engage in conversation. But, if an interview for publication is requested, he is known to turn off completely.

Jones was born in Arkabutla, Mississippi, on January 17, 1931, the son of actor Robert Earl and Ruth Jones. Before his birth, his father left the family to become first a prize-fighter and eventually an actor. After his parents divorced, his mother remarried and took him to live with his maternal grandparents, who lived on a farm near Manistee, Michigan. He was adopted by them and saw his mother only occasionally because she had to work as a tailor in neighboring towns.

On the farm, Jones hunted and fished and helped his grandparents with everyday chores. He took care of the livestock and learned masonry as a trade. He has told the press that moving north probably saved him from many of the pitfalls that confront a black youth in the South. He told *Newsweek,* "I've met lots of cousins who stayed in the South. I've always noticed a lack of assertiveness about them. It would have happened to me if I stayed, a certain self-castration."

Not long after he moved to Michigan, Jones developed a stammering problem so serious that he eventually could communicate only with his teacher and classmates by writing. Out of a strong will to overcome this impediment, he forced himself to join debating teams at high school. By the time of his graduation, he had completely overcome the handicap.

During this period, he discovered a picture of his father in a scene from *Strange Fruit* in an old copy of *Look* which impressed his classmates so much that he became a celebrity in school. On the day that he won both a public-speaking contest and a scholarship to college, he was given the money to call his father in New York. It took an hour of deliberating before he finally summoned up enough courage to make the call.

In 1949, Jones entered the University of Michigan, where he joined the drama group in a further effort to find his own identity. During the summer of his junior year, he went to New York to meet his father for the first time. Both engaged in a genuine effort to establish some kind of father–son relationship. Whether or not that effort achieved the expected results, both father and son shared one common interest—the theatre. They went to see the current plays together, and this provided Jones with his first exposure to the Broadway stage. Soon after Jones returned to college, where he had been pursuing a premedical course, he changed his major to drama and he was graduated with a B.A. in that subject.

After graduation, Jones entered the Army in order to fulfill his ROTC obligation. At first he was stationed at Fort Benning, Georgia, where he was thrown in with a group of Southern whites who, in his own words, "washed me out." He was transferred to the Cold Weather Training Command in Colorado, where he was exposed to skiing and mountain climbing, which made him at one time even consider making the Army a career.

Upon his release from the Army in 1955, he moved to New York City to live with his father. Under the GI Bill, he entered the American Theatre Wing where he studied acting with Lee Strasberg and Tad Danielewski and, after two years, he received a diploma. It was through an advertisement in a theatrical trade paper that he was led to his first small part in an off-Broadway show, *Wedding in Japan,* in 1957. One evening during the run he took over the lead role from Ivan Dixon, and an important theatrical agent just happened to be in the audience. She was impressed by him and signed him up.

From that time on, Jones was kept constantly working in the theater. For his performance in *Clandestine on the Morning Line* (1962) he received an Obie Award as best actor in the off-Broadway theatre. The same year he received the Theatre World Award as most promising personality for his part in *Moon on a Rainbow Shawl.* But honors alone were not enough and with the shockingly low salaries paid actors in most off-Broadway shows (averaging forty-five dollars a week), he could not make ends meet. In order to supplement his income, he often worked at polishing floors or making hero sandwiches in small food shops.

A turning point in both his professional and his personal life took place during the period when he was playing an important role in the long-running Jean Genêt play *The Blacks,* which opened in 1961 at the St. Mark's Playhouse. He told a reporter from the *Washington Post,* "In some ways that role in a powerful drama, that night after night forced me through all the hatred, disaffections and distrusts between white and black, was more real than the life I was leading. Through that role, I came to realize that the black man in America is the tragic hero, the Oedipus, the Hamlet, the Macbeth . . . even the working-class Willie Loman, the Uncle Tom and Uncle Vanya of contemporary American life."

This awareness of social commitment deepened over the years and was expressed most dramatically while Jones was in Spain filming *The Great White Hope* (1969). During that period, the Black Panthers were being harassed and even killed off and there was a great deal of unrest throughout the country. Instead of waiting to find out whether there was a conspiracy on the part of the police or not, Jones immediately wrote a check for $500 for the lawyers who were defending the Panthers.

He told Muriel Resnik of *New York* Magazine: "I am nothing without the Panthers, as a black man or a human being. I can't stand divisions any more and I certainly can't stand to contribute to them. I want unity and I want it all over. But I have to start in my own head, and my own family and my own race first. Just get your head straight no matter what bag you're in, right? That's my America."

It is the dream of most black actors to play the title role in Shakespeare's classic *Othello* at some time. Although he had appeared since 1960 in Joseph Papp's Shakespeare in the Park series, Jones did not get to play *Othello* until the summer of 1964. Even though Jones felt that he was still too young to fulfill the role completely at that time, he won such high critical acclaim that the production was moved that fall into an off-Broadway theatre, where it ran in repertory with *Baal* for almost a year. For his performances in both of these plays he was awarded the 1965 Obie Award as best actor off-Broadway.

It was during *Othello* that Jones met his wife, actress Julienne Marie, who played opposite him as Desdemona, but it was not until January 1967 that they actually got married. Although his wife has expressed her desire to continue her own career in the theatre, she does not wish to go on the road with a show. She told a *New York Post* reporter, "I don't like separations. Two weeks after we were married we were separated for three months. I wouldn't want to go through that again." The separation was, of course, due to professional commitments.

In those few intervals between plays, Jones has managed to do some work in films. Most notable, of course, was *The Great White Hope,* for which he was nominated for an Oscar in 1971 as best male actor. As early as 1963, he appeared in *Dr. Strangelove* with Peter Sellers, George C. Scott, and Sterling Hayden. Other films included *The Comedians* (1967), *The End of the Road* (1968), *The Man* (1972), and *Malcolm X* (1972).

His earliest appearance on television, in "East Side, West Side," won for him a nomination for an Emmy as well as the Golden Nymph Award in 1963. Other important programs on which he appeared were "The Defenders" (1964), "Dr. Kildare" (1965), "Tarzan" (1967 and 1968), and an NET Special, "Trumpets of the Lord" (1968). Early in 1973, Jones became the host-narrator on a new, nationally syndicated series entitled "Black Omnibus," which was highly praised by reviewers throughout the country.

During recent years, Jones has felt the need to expand his theatrical activities into the area of directing. His first attempt was as conceiver, codirector, and leading player in an all-black production of Chekhov's *The Cherry Orchard* (1972) at the New York Shakespeare Festival's Public Theatre. Although the reactions of the press, his colleagues, and audiences were varied, it was clear that a highly gifted artist was at work. Of one thing there is no question—James Earl Jones is one of the most important talents in the American theatre.

ARTHUR MITCHELL

First Black Ballet Star and Director, Dance Theatre of Harlem

WHEN HARLEM-BORN Arthur Mitchell joined the New York City Ballet in 1955, he became the first black dancer to become a member of a major ballet company. Since that time, he made a meteoric rise to the position of premier danseur and became the first black male classical ballet star. His electric performance as Puck in the company's *A Midsummer Night's Dream* was acclaimed by dance critic Walter Terry as "one of the great comedy portrayals of our day." From Moscow to Paris to New York, his appearances are frequently rewarded with standing ovations. His great concern for developing other black dancers into potential material for major ballet companies led him to interrupt his dancing career to establish Dance Theatre of Harlem and its associated school. In the following conversation, which took place in his office, he discussed his own career as a dancer and his hopes for his company.

ABDUL: Of what relevance is classical ballet to black kids and the black community?

MITCHELL: What blacks have to do now, aside from the thing of self-identity, is to get the technique with which to compete on an international basis in every area. To do just ethnic dancing is being so subjective that you can't compete. Now the strongest technical base of any form of dance that I know right now is classical ballet.

ABDUL: Like classical music. Many of the jazz musicians have had a classical background.

MITCHELL: Right. Take Nina Simone, who is supposed to be the mother of soul. She was a concert pianist at Juilliard before she started doing that. Once you have your classical background, you can become a tap dancer or an ethnic dancer, as far as I'm concerned. Katherine Dunham had a compulsory ballet class every morning before she had the ethnic class. And it is *that* discipline, training, and technique that I am giving the kids. If they want to go into another style, fine, but get your technical base. That's what I'm after. That is why I'm teaching them classical ballet, because it is the strongest technical base we know in the Western world. Personally, I don't teach ethnic dancing, because I've never studied it, but we teach ethnic dancing at the school.

ABDUL: Do you have any trouble getting boys to study ballet?

MITCHELL: I have no problems with this because we take the dance and make it relevant to the kids. We take social dancing, folk dancing, and break it down to classical steps. We show that all we've done is take folk or social dance and refine it to its furthest point and developed it into a technique so that we can reproduce it as many times as necessary. If you have to do eight shows a week, you can't go on just feeling or soul at that moment.

ABDUL: Not unless you are satisfied with an uneven performance.

MITCHELL: Exactly. If you take the arts, to which many young people have not been exposed, and talk about them in esoteric terms, they can't relate. But if you can put it into terms to which they can relate, then it is no problem. When it comes to boys, I show them how studying ballet can help them with their football, basketball, and other sports. By having a good demi-plié in classical dance, you can jump higher. *That,* they can understand.

ABDUL: It is amazing to me that within the short span of two years you were able to take relative beginners and develop a professional company.

MITCHELL: Necessity is the mother of invention. We are a nonprofit, tax-exempt organization. You have to match all the funds that you get and the matching of funds has to come from earned and unearned income. So, when you have to go out and earn the money, you have to give the public something. These kids don't come to the school because their parents bring them. They are here because *they* want to study, so they put in a good six, seven, eight hours, five, six, seven days a week.

ABDUL: How can they afford so many lessons?

MITCHELL: We only charge youngsters from seven to twelve a dollar a week and teen-agers two dollars a week, so they can come every day. The school itself is open to anyone who walks in the door and it is totally integrated. We've got Puerto Rican, Chinese, Caucasian. The company itself is all black because there was a theory that blacks could not do classical ballet. So that's why the company is all black, as it will remain until that theory is disproven and other companies begin to integrate on a very good basis. Anyone can come to the school to study whether he is talented or not. We think that any child should be able to study the arts whether or not he wants to become professional. This is also developing an audience which can appreciate what it is seeing.

ABDUL: When I saw the company at ANTA, I was impressed by the large number of young black people in the audience and how excited they were over the performance.

MITCHELL: That was because they were turned on by something. Anyone can relate to movement, and if it is done right, anyone can appreciate it. When you see these kids up there really giving their hearts and that discipline and training, you can't help but say it's good. You may not agree with the style, but you've got to say it's good.

ABDUL: I can remember when some of my friends were studying ballet and they had to pay a lot of money for training.

MITCHELL: Well, we're not in it to make money. We're here to give the arts to the community because everyone needs something in their lives to express whatever they feel inside. To become a professional is another thing. All we are saying is, "Here is a possibility for you." That's what we are trying to do. Then, we take the theoretically speaking "gifted" ones and gear them to become professionals. We give them a small living stipend of fifty to seventy-five dollars a week.

ABDUL: Within a short time you are going to have more trained dancers than the company can absorb.

MITCHELL: Right. We have already formed a junior performing company with about thirty kids.

ABDUL: Where do they perform?

MITCHELL: At high schools, camps, women's clubs. It gives the kids a chance to perform before audiences. They see what they are studying for and the fruition of all those classes. And they work on a stage. It's like on-the-job training. This provides a kind of training that you cannot get in the classroom.

ABDUL: They get the feel of an audience.

MITCHELL: And eventually we feel that Dance Theatre of Harlem will become one of the major companies of America. We feel it is *the* major young company now.

ABDUL: What are some of the considerations taken into account when you choose the repertoire for Dance Theatre of Harlem?

MITCHELL: We are working toward developing our own style. We will have things created especially for us, that goes without saying. At the same time, we are trying to develop young black choreographers, designers, etc., but the main thing is that, until we can do the masterworks, people will always think we are second. So, that's why we have Jerry Robbins's *Afternoon of a Faun,* Balanchine's *Agon* and *Concerto Barocco,* and John Harris's *Design for Strings.* And we are also working now to do *Giselle.* But we are changing the setting to Louisiana and making her a black slave girl, so it will make the story indigenous to us. It's like taking the classics and making them our own. Eventually, I hope to do something on *Othello* or take some of the classical characters of black history like Toussaint.

ABDUL: Now, about yourself. When did you decide you wanted to become a ballet dancer?

MITCHELL: I never actually decided. I was always a good social dancer. I went to Junior High #43 and at the class party I was dancing and the guidance teacher told me to try out for the High School of the Performing Arts. I wrote for the application and they said to prepare a three-minute dance routine. I had no formal training, so I found an old vaudeville performer named Tom Nit in the old CBS building and learned a tap routine to "Stepping Out with My Baby." They accepted me because boys were at a premium in the dance classes. After my first year, I was told I would never be a dancer. Well, I'm the kind of person who should never be told that I *can't* do something. The minute you tell me I *can't,* that's the moment I'm determined that I'm *going* to do it.

ABDUL: What is your astrological sign?

MITCHELL: I'm Aries. Nothing deters you. When I graduated, I was the first male to win the dance award. I won scholarships to Bennington College and to the School of the American Ballet. I decided that if I wanted to be a professional dancer, I should stay in New York in the hub of the training and action. So, I accepted the scholarship to the School of the American Ballet, which is the official school of the New York City Ballet. Lincoln Kirstein, who offered me the scholarship, told me, "If I take you into the school and into the company, you've got to be better than anybody else I've got just to get into the Corps de Ballet." I said, "You're on. That's the kind of challenge I like to have." He said, "Because you're black, you'll have to break down a lot of things." I said, "Fine!" I started studying ballet when I was eighteen and joined the company when I was twenty-one—that was after only three years of study.

ABDUL: Then you mastered the technique of ballet in a very short period of time. This puts you in a unique position to pass this on to other young people. I've always thought a lot of time is wasted during any kind of training.

MITCHELL: Exactly. We are finding that out now with the whole educational system. Before, the whole eighth-grade class used to have to go through the semester's work in the same length of time. Now, if a kid can do the whole thing in six months, then let him do it. You should make a youngster work at his maximum rather than at his minimum.

ABDUL: It must be rewarding to you to see the development your own students have made up to this point.

MITCHELL: Yes. The whole style and technique we're developing. It's like when Balanchine came from the Kirov School in Russia to America and took that style and technique and adapted it to American bodies. I'm taking the schooling I've had with Balanchine and adapting it to black bodies and utilizing our way, and we'll eventually get a whole different look. It will be classical, but it will have an added dimension.

ABDUL: Are you going to remain with the New York City Ballet?

MITCHELL: Officially, I'm not with any company now. But I do dance when I can and I am hoping to dance more starting now. We have our home established, so I'll have time to do more dancing myself.

CARMAN MOORE
Music Critic - Composer

$\mathcal{M}$USIC CRITIC, COMPOSER, WRITER, and teacher, Carman Moore was born in Lorain, Ohio, in 1936. He has earned a B.A. in music at Ohio State University and an M.A. at Juilliard in New York City. His reviews appear regularly in the *Village Voice* and he is a frequent contributor to *The New York Times*. He is also the author of *Somebody's Angel Child: The Story of Bessie Smith*. Although a critic is not an entertainer himself, he spends much of his time observing and commenting on performing artists. Therefore, I thought that the following conversation between Mr. Moore and myself would have considerable relevance to this book.

ABDUL: When did you get involved in writing about music?

MOORE: I had shown some plays and poems of mine to a playwright friend. His wife happened to be Mary Nichols, who writes political stuff for *The Village Voice*. They needed someone to write especially about twentieth-century music, so she recommended me.

ABDUL: So you've been writing for the *Voice* since 1965.

MOORE: Theoretically. Actually, I started writing about jazz and popular music around 1968 or so. Then in 1970, I started my column "New Time" so that I could deal with more subjects and at greater length.

ABDUL: And you've done record reviews for *The New York Times.*

MOORE: Both record reviews and feature articles. They've also asked me to do daily reviews, but I'm busy teaching also.

ABDUL: Where are you teaching?

MOORE: At Brooklyn College. I'm teaching everything from music theory to Afro-American music history.

ABDUL: I'd be interested in what you have to say about young people who are carrying on the jazz tradition. For example, who do you consider the young giants of jazz today? Herbie Hancock?

MOORE: Well, Herbie is a very important link between the kind of lyrical harmony-aware days of late bebop even though he's very young. In his head he is that kind of technician. At the same time, he's a link between that and the new kind of thing, which is more concerned with spontaneity and is more instantly involved with improvisation. The new thing is not about jazz treatment of tunes any more.

ABDUL: I'd like to know more about the people who are doing this highly improvisational thing. Suppose they do a piece entitled "Ode to Carman Moore" and they are called upon to do that same piece at another time. What happens when they do a repeat performance?

MOORE: Well, the fact that they do a piece means that there is a framework. They've decided they are going to do four notes in a certain way and do it very fast with everybody jamming and then come back to the four notes.

And, then they take off into the body of the piece.

ABDUL: So there is a formal structure?

MOORE: Oh, yes. But that structure is not based on a tune. That's one way to look at it. Or, they will set up a certain bass line and it will come again and again. They will play this riff over and over again. Over the top of that, they'll erect a piece.

ABDUL: Who are some of the performers you consider important?

MOORE: I've been very impressed by Don Cherry, who used to be the trumpet player with Ornette Coleman. And there's Milford Graves, the percussionist in the broadest sense of the word. He is currently writing a book about playing free. This is really for all instrumentalists. It is a collection of his observations of people who play that way and how they play that way—what they are aiming for. Even though he is one of the most important players of the new thing, he is highly critical of a lot of people who are getting away with just wiggling their valves on their horns.

ABDUL: And who else?

MOORE: Needless to say, Ornette Coleman is a leader in the field. He is a major influence. He has recently written a work for symphony orchestra, which I think is an important piece. And Marion Brown is way out on the edge of what will happen in the next few years. He is originally an alto saxophone player like Ornette—a disciple of Charlie Parker. But he has been creating entirely new instruments, he just makes whole rooms full of instruments.

ABDUL: How accessible is his music to the listener?

MOORE: He has recordings, but he isn't really with a company that will look after him yet. He has a piece called

"Afternoon of a Georgia Faun" in which he has the sound of rain falling and the whole piece is built up from there.

ABDUL: He sounds like he ought to be doing film scores, too.

MOORE: Oh, sure. He'll be out pretty soon. Right now, there are two things going on—the return to roots—that kind of soul thing is happening. At the same time, there's a very far-out thing happening. The current influence is James Brown and those basic riffs that his band plays show up throughout the jazz world. Like Miles Davis responded to it.

ABDUL: Then James Brown is an important influence?

MOORE: By all means. And that whole soul sound. The intensity of somebody like Wilson Pickett and the wilder ones who really set it out there. Their influence is really felt. There has been a return to a sense of the old harmonies. But Miles has mixed these elements. Herbie Hancock has mixed the elements. Sam Rivers is another person who I must mention. He plays tenor saxophone, flute—all of them. And he is a master of improvisation.

ABDUL: What are some of the problems facing the young jazz musician?

MOORE: The whole problem with jazz since Charlie Parker is that it got to be listening music. Before that, it was music to entertain people—music like Ellington used to play for reviews and the dance sets they did up at the Cotton Club and those places. Since Parker, the jazz player relies on the jazz fan to listen to his music in concert style.

ABDUL: What do you think the function of a jazz critic should be?

MOORE: First of all, I myself am not a *jazz* critic—I'm a

97

music critic. Just as I think that the players of the music of the future should learn to play in a lot of different styles, I think that the critic also has to be more wide-ranging so that he can deal with the twentieth century. In other words, there is no way in the world to know what Ornette Coleman is doing in "Skies of America" being a jazz critic because some of the references are to classical music.

ABDUL: Since the origins of jazz are basically black, do you feel that this music should be the sole domain of black people? How do you feel about white people exploiting it for profit?

MOORE: I think things should happen as they happen. There are several problems. One is that this country is still a racist country and this has its most devastating effects in the marketplace.

ABDUL: There are a large number of highly talented black people creating exciting things which are picked up by what I call "commercial" performers who exploit these things to the limit. The black creators go on creating great things and making very little money. Their works are rich and vital, while their imitators water down the material to make it more palatable to white tastes.

MOORE: That is where the whole world of white performers in rock becomes valid. Many white kids needed Janis Joplin's way of singing black music because they really couldn't catch all the nuances that Aretha Franklin or Sarah Vaughn or somebody like that would be laying down.

ABDUL: I always felt that Janis Joplin was trying to force something out of herself that wasn't really there. Whereas with Aretha, it just seems to flow from her naturally.

MOORE: The important thing is the gift. I think that there are several factors. Black musicians and black music have borrowed heavily from white music, too. They have used things where they want to. Certainly all of those Motown strings are taken from the white symphony orchestra.

ABDUL: Are you saying that it is a cultural exchange, that music belongs to everybody?

MOORE: Black music has become a worldwide phenomenon. The fact that there are rock groups in Japan is significant.

ABDUL: Some people say that all popular music forms are simply jazz reappearing in different guises.

MOORE: I don't quite subscribe to that. Jazz music has to be instrumental music, even though it may pattern itself on the human voice. To me, it is instrumental music and it's pretty abstract. Whereas, popular music—the vocal forms—are another bag.

ABDUL: Who are the outstanding exponents today of black popular music?

MOORE: The obvious ones are Ray Charles and Aretha Franklin.

ABDUL: These are the giants. And how do you classify Roberta Flack?

MOORE: She's going to be. Also, an absolute giant who nobody pays much attention to is Esther Phillips.

ABDUL: And she was brought to our attention by the program "Soul!"

MOORE: The best popular singer in the world is Sarah Vaughn. She's a classic. And she's come back singing in the style she's not supposed to know. She's just absolutely wiped everybody out, she's so incredible.

ABDUL: What about the male vocalists?

MOORE: There aren't too many giants right now.

ABDUL: There's Al Green.

MOORE: He's going to be.

ABDUL: Of course his style is so special, I'm just wondering how long one will want to listen to something that limited. And there's Michael Jackson who, with Al Green, had four records in one year which sold over a million copies. What about the future of a Michael Jackson?

MOORE: I think he is going to become a giant. I see the indications there.

ABDUL: As long as his voice doesn't change the wrong way. If it changes and he doesn't have a voice any more, wow!

MOORE: I also think that Stevie Wonder is important.

ABDUL: He is beginning to go way out. He's using the Moog Synthesizer. He's really a highly gifted young performer.

MOORE: Wilson Pickett is also a marvelous performer. The two geniuses of the last thirty years of black popular music have died—Sam Cooke and Otis Redding. Otis Redding was going to be *so* dominant in the world of music. These giants are able to sing chorus after chorus after chorus and not repeat themselves, which is a jazz function.

ABDUL: Getting back to our giants who are *now* living and performing. Let's establish who they are.

MOORE: Well, the women are Aretha Franklin, Esther Phillips, Nina Simone, and Sarah Vaughn. Of the men,

Ray Charles is the king. I have to put James Brown in there because he has created a style that has had great influence. He's tied Africa to the U.S. in a very viable way. And Wilson Pickett. That's about it.

RON O'NEAL

Actor

SYMBOLIC OF THE new generation of film stars, Cleveland-born Ron O'Neal became an overnight sensation when he dazzled the movie-going public with his performance as Priest in *Super Fly*. Unlike most of his colleagues, he does not come from the world of sports with no previous theatrical training. O'Neal served a long apprenticeship in the legitimate theater, which included eight years at Cleveland's famous Karamu Theatre, where he played nearly forty different roles. For his performance in the New York company of *No Place to be Somebody* (a Pulitzer Prize winner), O'Neal won the Drama Desk, Theater World, Clarence Derwent and Obie awards. He received high critical acclaim for his performances in both the East and West Coast productions of *Dream on Monkey Mountain*. In this conversation, which took place in his New York apartment, O'Neal speaks candidly about his movie career, his beginnings in the theatre, and his hopes for the future.

ABDUL: When you did *Super Fly* did you have any idea that it would be the success it turned out to be?

O'NEAL: I thought the story was going to be a great commercial success. But because of the nature of the production—the limited budget—I was very worried about the film, and I really thought it had to be one of the worst films ever made. That was my feeling as an actor working in the film.

ABDUL: You actually ran out of film at one time, didn't you?

O'NEAL: Right. On one occasion we actually stopped for about ten days because there simply was *no* film and *no* money. I was never paid really through the shooting of *Super Fly* at all. It was a question of paying me or paying the cameraman.

ABDUL: Without the cameraman there would have been no film.

O'NEAL: I wasn't working for the few hundred dollars a week in salary that I was to get while shooting the film. I was working for the artistic success that my career needed. I just stuck in there so the cameras would keep rolling. It was one of those rare films that wasn't approached from a Hollywood point of view.

ABDUL: There were many little nuances that made it real.

O'NEAL: I thought so. I think the movie went over a lot of people's heads. It was never our intention to beat anyone over the head with a moral because it wasn't that kind of film. The purpose on my part was to depict truthfully the life style of a person like Priest—which I think the film largely succeeded in doing.

ABDUL: How did you get the idea for *Super Fly?*

O'NEAL: Actually it was suggested by an article on drug pushers and a friend of mine from Cleveland, Phil Fenty, came to me with the idea of writing a screenplay for me. We talked about it for many weeks and started to write it.

We had the body of the story line completed and two or three scenes written out and he came up with the producer, Sig Shore.

ABDUL: When did you decide to become an actor?

O'NEAL: I had never seen a live stage production until I was twenty. I had just left Ohio State University after two disastrous courses and I was sort of bumming around in Cleveland and a friend of mine took me to Karamu Theatre. Like most black people in Cleveland, I had never been there before—the production was *Finian's Rainbow*. Up until that time, I had been exposed to all the normal professions, but nothing turned me on.

ABDUL: You didn't care for school?

O'NEAL: No. I was only there two-quarters—enough to get the lay of the land. I'm really a curious sort of person because I'm sort of half ghetto—not enough to incapacitate me, but enough to keep me honest—and half middle class.

ABDUL: The important thing is that these forces don't work against each other.

O'NEAL: Well, I can move easily back and forth. I went to school with doctors' daughters and also cats that ultimately went to the electric chair. From one extreme to the other. My neighborood was like that—the Glenville area. I'd stand on the corner and watch all the hustlers right around the corner from the Tiajuana. That used to be *the* place. All the Cadillacs, the Mercury Bar, Gold Coast, and Riley's Pool Hall. . . . Anyway, I went to see *Finian's Rainbow* in the spring of 1957 and when the theatre reopened in the fall, I got into the chorus of *Pajama Game,* which starred Al Fann. I did only musicals for about three years. And I studied dance. I wasn't doing well at it because I was too muscular, too big, and it was too late for me to start dancing.

ABDUL: It didn't hurt you, did it?

O'NEAL: No, it helped my acting tremendously—my body movement. After three years I still hadn't done a major role and I was getting a little frustrated, so I moved to drama.

ABDUL: Did you get better roles?

O'NEAL: Yes. One of the things I did was *Summer of the Seventeenth Doll* with Dorothy Silver.

ABDUL: She's a marvelous director. She can take people who have had very little experience and make them look like professionals on stage.

O'NEAL: It's true, she's a very talented lady. I did either strong supporting or major roles until 1966, when I was invited to come to New York and teach acting at HARYOU Act.

ABDUL: Did you enjoy the teaching experience?

O'NEAL: I found it rewarding but frustrating. It was not nearly so much with the students, but with HARYOU Act itself and the structure that I had to work in. I found that no one was concerned with the welfare of the kids.

ABDUL: Did you ever formally study acting?

O'NEAL: I learned to act on my own. After you have done as many plays as I did—I must have been in forty plays—with any kind of interest, you learn something about acting. Unlike many of the people at Karamu, I didn't *play* in the productions, so I suppose I wasn't easy to get along with for that reason. I think that acting sort of chose me. All I ever had to do was to consider the alternatives.

ABDUL: What were the alternatives?

O'NEAL: Well, I could continue to be a house painter in Shaker Heights or I could go back to some of the factories I worked in.

ABDUL: But that didn't happen. What did you do after Haryou Act?

O'NEAL: I took a leave of absence because it occurred to me that I didn't have an Equity card. So I did summer stock. I put a rag on my head and did the chorus of *Showboat*.

ABDUL: Did you have to put on dark makeup or did they recognize the fact that blacks come in all colors?

O'NEAL: They were so desperate for tenors that they didn't care what color I was, although they did say, "Tie a rag around your head and hide your hair." [Ron O'Neal has straight hair]. And that's another thing I wouldn't do again.

ABDUL: Has the fact that you are light-complexioned with straight hair been a drawback in getting roles?

O'NEAL: Absolutely.

ABDUL: Producers have always had a certain black prototype in their minds which seems impossible to change.

O'NEAL: They thought that is the way it should be. After *Super Fly* nothing could be more clear that it is not that way, and you can expect a rash of light-skinned actors now. Raymond St. Jacques cast one in *Book of Numbers*.

ABDUL: Well, Raymond St. Jacques knows what is really happening.

O'NEAL: Whether the producer is black or white has nothing to do with it. Black people have been equally guilty of the same discrimination, at least in my experience. I have been turned down by almost an equal number of black producers. It is doubtful that I would have ever gotten *Super Fly* if it had gone through conventional channels.

ABDUL: At one point, you had hopes of becoming an opera singer. What happened to those hopes?

O'NEAL: I really started too late and it would have taken a kind of dedication. You can't stay out late and you have that awful paranoia that tenors go through about colds and their voices. The voice is such a fickle and delicate thing and I just didn't think it was worth it. I'd much rather be a first-rate actor than a third-rate tenor.

ABDUL: Do you think that someday you might like to stage an opera?

O'NEAL: Possibly. I'd like to put some *soul* into opera. The music is full of soul. We are such a completely musical and dramatic people. If you could erase whatever antagonism from the initial response to the music—black people have a tremendous affinity toward Italian opera.

ABDUL: Now that you have done both *Super Fly* and *Super Fly T.N.T.*, what course are you going to follow in your career?

O'NEAL: Well, it's already moving into direction. I coauthored the script of *Super Fly T.N.T.*, starred in it, and directed it. So I'm moving into direction and production. I own a piece of both films and they will provide me with the money to do some of the things that I have always wanted to do.

ABDUL: Would you like to return to the stage?

O'NEAL: I have very bad feelings about the stage. I would like to do a play simply to heal the wounds and to get my acting back together—to do a total performance—to sharpen up the instrument. But the problem with the stage is that you have to wait several years before you get a play worth doing.

ABDUL: What do you think about the group of so-called black leaders who want to start a censorship board which would decide whether films project the right images of black people?

O'NEAL: Black films go through the same censorship board that white films go through and get a rating. Now I think that any group of people who would presume to be able to judge what is fit for black people to see should be institutionalized. I have starred in movies and also directed, so I guess that qualifies me as some kind of expert in the field. But I would no more consider sitting on such a board than the man on the moon. I would never presume to try to judge for a rural Southern black, a sophisticated New York black, a sun-worshipping California black—I would not presume to judge what films should be offered to the black population. If anyone would dare do such a thing, they should be checked out psychologically.

DIANA ROSS
Singer-Actress

SHE FAILED TO win a part in her high school musical play. She signed up for a vocal class at school and quit because she was afraid that she would not do well. She was a skinny little girl name Diane. And she became known to the whole world as Diana Ross.

Diana's childhood home was a third-floor walkup in the Detroit black ghetto. Her father was a laborer who worked himself up to foreman and was an active member in his union local. Her mother worked in white homes as a domestic. Diana had two sisters and three brothers, and they slept three in a bed in the same room.

But they were happy children. Nobody told them that they were poor and lived in a ghetto. Diana recalls: "If I wanted a penny or a nickel, I could always get a penny or a nickel. That's all Bazooka bubble gum and Quirrel candy cost, and I never wanted any more."

Christmas was a very special day in the Ross household. Diana's mother and father made sure that all the children received gifts on this occasion. One year, bicycles.

Singing was always a part of Diana's life. On Sundays she sang hymns at the Baptist church, later as a member of the choir. One night when Diana was six years old, her mother gave a party and Diana sang "In the Still of the

Night." A hat was passed and enough was raised to buy her a pair of black patent-leather shoes. She was very proud of those shoes!

But there were bad times too. Mrs. Ross became ill with tuberculosis and had to spend a long time away from her family in a sanitorium. Diana was sent to her grandparents in Alabama, where she lived for two years. While living in the South, Diana had to learn to use the back doors of white homes. "It didn't bother me," Diana says. She has always looked on the bright side of things.

When Mrs. Ross returned home from the sanitorium, the family was happily reunited. And this time they had a new home in a housing project called the Brewster-Douglass Houses.

Diana started high school, and she recalls that, for a short while, she didn't seem to mix very well and was not invited to parties. One thing she did enjoy was making dresses. Mrs. Ross would bring home discarded dresses from the lady for whom she worked and Diana would remodel them on the school sewing machine. Later, she began to design her own dresses and her high school class voted her "Best Dressed Girl."

After school and on weekends, Diana worked as a bus girl in the cafeteria at Hudson's Department Store. She was the first black to hold such a job—in those days blacks were kept in the kitchen away from the customers. People used to come to the cafeteria just to see the one black girl. Diana made it a point to be well groomed at all times so that she would make a good impression. Every Saturday afternoon, she attended the charm school at Hudson's. Another activity she liked was sports, and few boys could beat her at running or swimming.

But what interested her most was singing. She grew up during the years that rock music (then usually called rock 'n' roll) was developing. It was a part of her and she loved it. She was singing rock on street corners with other boys and girls when she was twelve and thirteen. Later, in high school, she joined two of her friends, Florence Ballard and Mary Wilson, and formed a singing group. They called themselves the Primettes.

Their professional debut took place one night in a ghetto back yard when they sang "My Cheating Heart." The hat was passed and the "take" was almost three dollars. Entertainment history was made that night because the Primettes only a few years later became the Supremes.

The girls sang wherever they could find an audience. They sang at record hops and all kinds of parties. Diana's father didn't approve. She recalls that she was sometimes whipped for appearing at those parties, but she continued to go all the same. "We sang because we loved to sing," she says. "We didn't care if we got paid."

The kids at school started noticing her. She found out that "if you think you're somebody, you *are* somebody." The girl who didn't get invited to parties was now one of the most popular girls in school. "When I walked down the school hall," she recalls, "I'd say 'Hi Bob,' 'Hi Timmy.' I must have said 'hi' a thousand times. I had so many friends."

Soon the Primettes were ready, they thought, for the next step in their careers. They wanted to make recordings. They had heard of a new record company, Motown, which was using talent discovered in the Detroit ghetto.

The man behind it was Berry Gordy, Jr., a black who only a few years earlier had been an assembly-line worker in an automobile plant. Knowing the huge success the girls were to become on the Motown label, one would think that their first meeting with Gordy would be sort of world-shaking. Far from it—the girls sang and he told them to go back to school. That was all!

But the girls, especially Diana, didn't give up that easily. They tried all sorts of ways to get Gordy interested in them. One story is that Diana got a job as an assistant to his secretary. Every time Gordy opened the door of his office, she would start to sing. Maybe that is why she was soon fired. But persistence paid off and the Primettes were engaged as background chorus on recordings of established Motown groups and Gordy soon put them into an intensive artist's development course.

"We learned," Diana recalls, "how to sit, how to walk, how never to open a door but let your escort do it. Even how to hold a cigarette." The way Diana sees it now, "We were just insecure kids, but Berry saw something in us, maybe that we weren't afraid of hard work." Whatever it was, Gordy gave them a chance to do a record of their own. And he named them the Supremes.

Neither that first record nor the eight singles that followed were a hit. Meantime, while waiting for that magic big record that would make them famous, the girls were sent on tour. With other Motown performers, they did one-night stands all over the South.

As the tour continued, something strange began to happen. When the Supremes, who had been unknown, were introduced, there was whistling and cheering. What had happened was that one of the records they made before leaving on the tour had caught on. It was called "Where Did Our Love Go?" By the time they got back to Detroit, they had become celebrities.

But fame meant even harder work. They had to meet disk jockeys, talk with public relations people, work on costumes, wigs, stage routines. And there was the endless traveling. "Have you ever spent twenty-one days on a bus," asks Diana, "keeping dates, keeping your wardrobe, your makeup, your wigs, singing one-nighters, longer engagements, up at 6 A.M. and back on that bus?"

The girls were well chaperoned. They had no boyfriends and were not allowed to go out alone. "We had no chance to make friends outside of the group of maybe twelve who traveled with us," recalls Diana.

"Like Europe. I've been to Europe many times, but Europe to me is just a stage door in Milan, a stage in London, a theatre some place else. We never had time to see anything, to feel where we were and what was different about it."

Musically, the sixties was the decade of the Beatles and the Supremes. The special sound of the Supremes came to be called "the Motown sound." What was its special quality? Remembering her childhood, Diana once said it was made up of "roaches, rats, and lots of love."

Some people criticized the Supremes for lack of soul. Diana's answer is that "we didn't try to sound white. We didn't try to sound black. My purpose was and is to make audiences happy." But she adds, "Always, we've tried to make people know that black people are beautiful people, not just physically but in heart and mind." They did this not only by the way they sang and the way they looked, but also by the way they lived. Each of the girls bought a home for their families and Diana sent her younger brothers and sisters to college.

In that fabulous decade of the Supremes, they sold twenty-five million records. They once had seven Number One records in a row and they had more gold records than any group with the exception of the Beatles. They appeared on television many times—in fact, actually, twenty-five times in one hectic year.

As the years went on, Diana, who had been the lead singer almost from the first, began to emerge as what one writer called "The Supreme *Supreme*." And so, the group began to be billed as Diana Ross and the Supremes. Diana also began to do solo appearances, most notably on a TV special called "Like Hep" with Lucille Ball and Dinah Shore. And then in January 1970 at Las Vegas, Diana Ross and the Supremes sang together for the last time.

Now she was on her own. This new phase of her career started with a very successful TV special simply entitled "Diana!" Then came engagements at the most fashionable night spots around the country such as Caesar's Palace in Las Vegas and the Waldorf-Astoria in New York.

One night at the Waldorf, a film producer heard her. He owned the rights for a film on the life of Billie Holiday and he was looking for someone to play the role of the great blues singer. Then and there he decided that the search was over. By a strange coincidence, Diana had already become interested in Billie Holiday and had listened to her records and studied her career and had even thought that maybe someday there might be a film!

When Diana was a child, her mother used to play Billie's records. But to Diana, rock was the thing and "Billie Holiday was nowhere when I was a kid."

"The first time I heard a Billie Holiday record, I thought, 'What's so great about Billie Holiday?' I wasn't into jazz. I didn't really care about her until I did research on her, until I began to hear snatches of people's memories of her."

After Diana was signed to play the role, the real work of preparation began. "What I did with Billie Holiday's music was live with it over a nine-month period. I just listened to it. I didn't in any way try to sound like her or phrase anything like her. Her music got to me by osmosis, I guess. It just came into my body by living with it and playing it constantly."

Diana looked upon the script as "just a clue to me of what really was supposed to happen. I had to go between the lines. I had to understand the actual feeling behind the words." Her technique was to write notes to herself. "I've always been a woodshedder," she says, "a person who goes off alone and thinks things out and practices and is ready when the lights come on me."

And when the camera lights were turned on the first day of shooting, Diana, as always, was ready. She had never acted before, and here she was not only the lead but practically the whole picture. There were 168 separate scenes, almost all involving her. She worked twelve hours a day for forty-one of the forty-two days she was needed on the set. She wore forty-three different costumes, from cast-off sweaters to beautiful stage gowns. She insisted that the first batch of costumes be thrown out and she herself supervised the design of the costumes she finally wore.

"Another thing I insisted on," says Diana, "was that where a black person could serve almost as well as a white, we use him. The unions said blacks weren't hired because they didn't have the experience. Well, if they weren't hired, how could they get the experience? The film was beautifully integrated. We had thirty-seven black people behind the scenes and thirty whites." Of sixty-four speaking roles, thirty-four were played by blacks and thirty by whites.

The result of all this work was *Lady Sings the Blues*. The film opens with a shot of Diana Ross, the superstar of the supper clubs, as a raggedy teen-ager hopscotching her way along a ghetto street in Baltimore. You believe that, just as you believe everything that follows in the tortured life of Billie Holiday: the struggle to become a singer, the frustrations of the one-night stands in the South which lead to her first use of drugs, the brief periods of success and luxury and love, the return to drugs, and, finally, a triumphant moment when she sings at Carnegie Hall.

The polished, glamorous lead singer of the Supremes, the epitome of pop art, had turned out to be a real actress. She surprised almost everyone including, she admits, herself. The critics acclaimed her and huge audiences came to see her. She received numerous awards. The most important was her nomination for an Oscar as best actress.

Today, Diana Ross is at the top of the entertainment world. She began with a natural singing voice, but it was hard work that put her where she is. "If I'm going to do something," she says, "then it's going to be the right thing because I'm going to work with everything I've got to make it right." She adds, "I think there are only two kinds of people in the world—winners and losers, and you're one or the other because of the image you have of yourself. . . . I won't let myself lose."

Her success has given her all the material things anyone could want. But it also has placed an obligation upon her. "I feel I have a duty to a lot of youngsters—to give them inspiration to show that they can get out of poverty and do something in their lives. Maybe I am some kind of symbol for the black girl. Men and women, white and black, all of them respect me, and that's because I respect myself. I think in doing this, I just help other black girls respect themselves, too."

Diana Ross, a millionaire at twenty-five, a superstar at thirty, might so easily have been spoiled by success, but she has kept her feet on the ground. "There's not a day that goes by that I don't look around my beautiful new home, at my husband and my two babies, and think, it's real and it's true and it's happened to me."

CICELY TYSON
Actress

ALTHOUGH HARLEM-BORN Cicely Tyson had a distinguished career on stage and in television, it was her remarkable portrayal of Rebecca in the film *Sounder* which elevated her to stardom and won her an Academy Award nomination as best actress in 1973. Beginning her acting career in the Vinnette Carroll production of *Dark of the Moon* at the Harlem YMCA, she won the Vernon Rice Award for her performance in *The Blacks* as well as *Moon on a Rainbow Shawl*. On Broadway, she won acclaim in *Tiger, Tiger Burning Bright* and *A Hand Is on the Gate*. She costarred with George C. Scott in the television series "East Side, West Side," for which she won an NAACP Image Award as best dramatic actress on television. While she was a top fashion model, Miss Tyson helped introduce the natural hairdo. In this conversation, which took place in her suite at the Park Lane Hotel, Miss Tyson discusses the film *Sounder,* her attitudes on the black image in film, and her advice to young people who aspire toward a film career.

ABDUL: You have received much acclaim for what has been called by critics the first black heroine on the screen in *Sounder*. How did you happen to get the part?

TYSON: Well, I *read* for it. I heard that they were doing a movie based on a novel, so I had my agent contact the producer. He told me that I would have to read for the part. My whole feeling about auditions is that you can't really tell anything because generally the actor is so nervous. I'm always surprised that I can get my mouth open because I'm always trying to swallow that lump. I explained that to him and he said, "Yes, we'll take all that into consideration and so when would you like to come?" He completely ignored everything I had said. Anyway, they set up a date and I guess I was the first one that day. This was nine-thirty in the morning and I thought that they sure wanted to get me out of the way. When I arrived about fifteen minutes early, the producers were not there. I panicked. I'll never forget the feeling that I had. I felt that I had become stone.

ABDUL: Wasn't there anyone there for you to talk to?

TYSON: There was a girl in the office when I arrived and she said, "Oh, there's nobody here, yet," and then she disappeared. So I sat on a couch in the corner. And I felt as if I had been frozen in that position, and that if anyone came and said anything to me that I would never be able to answer. I will never forget it. Finally, I guess it was Bob Radnitz who came in first with his dog. He nodded and went into his office. Then the girl came in and said, "Mr. Ritt's around here somewhere." She went out to get hold of him and they invited me into the office. And *they* talked. *I* didn't say a word. I decided that I was going to save everything—if there was anything there—until I read the scene. So I read the scene with the storekeeper with Bob. He got so excited. He walked around the room. But Martin Ritt simply sat there like the stone I thought I was, like a Buddha—he never said a word. Finally, he said, "We don't have to read you for the teacher because we know you can do that." I said, "I don't want to do the teacher simply because you know I can do her. I would like to do Rebecca because she is a challenge to me." And I added, "As an actress, I can only grow if I do things that you consider out of my range." He went on to say that I was too young, too pretty—all of those things. Then he said, "Well, we're going to read several other actresses and we'll see." It took two months of praying and meditating and finally one day I received a call from my agent. He said, "Well, it's yours!" I answered, "When do we go to work?" He asked, "Aren't you excited?" And I said, "No. I knew it was mine all along. I was just waiting for *you* to find out."

ABDUL: Sometimes you instinctively know when the vibrations are right.

TYSON: Absolutely. I never thought for one moment that she didn't belong to me. I felt that woman in every bone in my body. She was so much a part of me that, before I even got the official word, I started working on her.

ABDUL: Did you pattern the role on your own mother?

TYSON: Of course there is some of my own mother in her and there's a lot of Nana. Nana was an older lady who used to take care of us when my mother had to work. When I think back on my life, practically every black woman I knew had Rebecca in her. That kind of devotion to the children. That's why it was important for me to do Rebecca, because of all the black women that I had known in my life—the ones who gave me the kind of love that Rebecca gave those children. And the ones who had that kind of pride. The back that never bent—strong as an ox. It didn't matter about the size. They were a little concerned that I wasn't big enough for the role.

ABDUL: It would have been a mistake to cast a large woman in that role.

TYSON: Absolutely. As I was saying, Nana was a tiny woman. She must have been about four feet tall and wiry—but with the strength of an ox. So I knew that she did not have to be big and fat. As a matter of fact, nobody would have believed the truth that that family had no food. As I read the script, I felt the *pride,* the *strength,* the *dignity* in her. I felt the love and all the warmth that woman had. I knew that I could do it.

ABDUL: I know that you are concerned with the black woman and her image on the screen, but I think that the *father* is important in his own way. He disproves the myth that sociologists have tried to make us believe that black children do not receive love from their fathers.

TYSON: The thing that I found disturbing about the original book—I'm sure that I would not have done the film if they had not made this change—is that the father dies. My feeling about that was that for generations there is this myth that the black household lacks a male figure. I felt it was important that the male figure be put back into it. I talk so much about Rebecca because it struck me that here, for the first time since I can remember, is a black heroine in a film. Besides, there was a unity within that family that I had never seen projected on the screen before. The relationship between Nathan and Rebecca is unique. The film is very positive in all areas. It deals with us as human beings. And that is the greatest thing about

Sounder. Everybody can identify with it regardless of race, creed, color, or sex.

ABDUL: Do you feel that films have an influence on young people?

TYSON: Of course they do. It is ridiculous for anybody to say that they don't. I went down to watch the shooting of a movie Paul Winfield was doing under Ossie Davis's direction. It was very cold. And a lot of kids were standing around watching and talking. And I overheard one of them talking about *Super Fly.* I asked this little girl, "How old are you?" She answered, "Thirteen." I asked, "What do you know about *Super Fly*?" She answered, "I saw it." I told her, "You are not supposed to see those kinds of movies. There is a law that says that you are not supposed to." She said, "Well, I don't know, but I saw it." Then, I began to talk to her about it and she said, "Well, I was glad when he beat that man up and got all that money. . . ." Then she nudged her friend and said, "And how about that scene where he sniffed that cocaine." Now what is that for kids to be talking about?

ABDUL: That was really a great job of acting. I couldn't believe that this was the same Ron O'Neal from Karamu Theatre. There is nothing about Ron O'Neal like that character.

TYSON: But Ron O'Neal is a consummate actor. He's a brilliant actor. I have seen him do several things on stage. Despite the fact that people were putting down *Super Fly,* it took that film to make him rich. It took *Super Fly* to bring him to the attention of the public so that he could work more. It took a *Super Fly* to get him fifteen minutes on "The Dick Cavett Show." And that's a reality. But, by the same token, when you walk by the supermarket and an eight year old is singing the theme song and knows *all* the lyrics, tell me if that's not affecting youth.

ABDUL: The disturbing thing is that the kid understood exactly what the lyrics meant.

TYSON: Some people say it's not reality, that it's fantasy and all that, but children don't know the difference. And children are looking desperately for something to hold on to. And, it's a destruction of the whole black race as far as I'm concerned to give them those kinds of images.

ABDUL: If a young person came to you and said that they wanted to go into films, what would you say to them?

TYSON: I wouldn't *encourage* them, but I wouldn't *discourage* them, either. It's an extremely difficult thing. Because we've been able to make a dent in the movie industry, it looks as if there is a future for black films. But I think that we cannot afford to be led up the garden path. I get the feeling when I go around that many of the young people feel that they've got everything coming to them, that you don't have to work for it. That's a big mistake. If you manage to get in just out of sheer luck, then you'd better be prepared to stay there. It's like Vinnette Carroll [a New York director] said recently, "There are no kids around like the batch that came along with you. These kids don't want to *work*."

ABDUL: It's strange that you should mention Vinnette, because the first time I ever heard about you was when you did *Dark of the Moon* with her at the Harlem YMCA.

TYSON: I told somebody in an interview that Vinnette was the best teacher I ever had. She was so cruel and hard on me. I remember once going up for a role in a movie that Harry Belafonte was doing—just a bit part—but you know that at the beginning of a career every little thing is important. They hadn't given me a definite answer so I thought that I didn't get the part. When I told Vinnette, she lit into me: "You know, that's what is wrong with pretty girls. You rely on beauty and you don't learn your craft. In order to survive in this business, you've got to learn your *craft* and then you have something other than your beauty that makes you richer." I was so hurt because I was busy working hard at developing myself as an artist. When she told me that, I cried for days. About two weeks later, I got a call telling me that I got the part. And I told her, "See, you were *wrong*. It's just that they weren't ready. I had it all along." Well, recently she came to a screening of *Sounder* and she said, "I have never seen a performance on the screen like that by any actress black or white." And she said, "Where did you get the security to be able to play a role like that—without all the glamour, without all the fine clothes, without the hairdos, the makeup—how were you able to do that?" I just looked at her and laughed. In fact, I got hysterical. I said, "How could *you* ask me such a question? You who are forever telling me that women should not rely on their beauty, but should try to develop their craft—how can *you* be asking *me* such a question?"

MELVIN VAN PEEBLES
Writer - Composer - Filmmaker

IT IS HARD to label Chicago-born Melvin Van Peebles. Besides being a composer, filmmaker, playwright, producer, and director, he is also a novelist writing in both French and English. He first came to national attention with his motion picture *The Story of a Three-Day Pass,* which was called the first feature-length film to be directed by a black American released through commercial channels. This was followed by *Watermelon Man* and the spectacular box-office hit *Sweet Sweetback* and *Don't Play Us Cheap.* On Broadway, he stirred up a great deal of controversy with his plays *Ain't Supposed to Die a Natural Death* and *Don't Play Us Cheap* (stage version).

Born on the South side of Chicago, Van Peebles grew up in Phoenix, Illinois, where he attended Thornton Township High School. He has told the press of his youth: "I must have been a little strange even as a kid, with my nose stuck in a book all the time." He had a reputation for reading many books and he used to get beat up frequently for not belonging to the neighborhood gang.

He furthered his education at West Virginia State College and, after the first years, he transferred to Ohio Wesleyan, from which he was graduated in 1953 with a B.A. in English Literature. After three and a half years in the Air Force, he tried painting in Mexico, then moved to San Francisco.

In San Francisco, Van Peebles earned his living by working as a grip man on a cable car. This inspired him to write the text for a picture book entitled *The Big Heart,* which was published in 1957. In it, he said, "I like being a grip man. Sometimes as the cable car goes by I see my reflection in a store window and I fool myself and tell myself I'm not really me, but a ghost from the past." For some reason he was fired by the company in spite of the fact that he had never been late or absent from the job. When he went to the FEPC to protest his being fired, they asked him if anyone had called him a "nigger." Since the answer was negative, they asked him how he could call it discrimination, and the matter was dropped.

After unsuccessful attempts to break into the film industry in Hollywood, where the only job he could get was sweeping floors, he packed up his household (which included a wife and children) and moved to Europe. With his GI Bill, he studied astronomy in the Netherlands and managed to get a role in the Dutch National Theatre's production of Brendan Behan's *The Hostage.*

He moved on to Paris, where he supported himself by singing and dancing outside of theatres and writing for French periodicals. In spite of the fact that he was constantly moving in and out of various apartments, Van Peebles managed to write and publish five novels. Only *A Bear for the F.B.I.* was written in English, after which he was able to write directly into French without the aid of a translator. His other books include *The Chinaman of the 14th District, The True American, The Party in Harlem,* and *La Permission.*

His novel *La Permission* became the basis for the screen-play for his film *The Story of a Three-Day Pass*. It was this script which served as the proper credential to qualify him to take the examination for directors at the French Film Center to make him eligible for a $60,000 subsidy for films that are "artistically valuable, but not necessarily commer-cially viable."

He was lucky enough to find a small producing com-pany, O.P.E.R.A., to produce it. Van Peebles recalls, "I ac-tually shot the film in six weeks for $200,000. That's noth-ing for a movie. When I'm filming, I'm alone. I run a tight ship. I tell them what I want and say, 'Give me that; do what you got to do first and talk to me about it later.' I ran the cutting room, I ran the music, I ran the thing. That can't be done in the American system."

At a party in Paris, Van Peebles got caught in a conver-sation with another black American, Albert Johnson, who, it turned out, was a program director for the San Francisco International Film Festival. They got their heads together and the end result was an invitation for Van Peebles to show *The Story of a Three-Day Pass* as the French entry at the festival in 1967.

Because of its success in San Francisco, the film was brought into New York the following July and was most enthusiastically received by *Saturday Review's* erudite critic, Hollis Alpert. He wrote that it was "so pleasantly and sin-cerely made, so filled with delightful touches of humour, and for a first effort, so surprisingly adept technically." *The Village Voice* added, "Peebles shows talent and in-telligence above and beyond the demands of tokenism."

In an interview with Judy Stone in *The New York Times*,

Van Peebles said, "There is a certain awareness I must have, being a Negro director, but even if I'm intrigued by a Negro subject, I won't do that for my next film. I don't want to get typecast like Negro writers are typecast."

But the big Hollywood studio Columbia Pictures beckoned, and Van Peebles signed a contract to do *Watermelon Man* (1970), a satire about a white bigot who turns black. The studio had the preconceived notion to cast a white actor in the role, but Van Peebles fought with them relentlessly until they finally gave the part to Godfrey Cambridge. After the film got the Van Peebles treatment, the producer protested that he had filmed it from a *black* point of view! In its review of the film, *The New York Times* wrote, "Saddest of all, and 'Watermelon Man' is a sad occasion, is the waste of an able new director, Melvin Van Peebles."

To avoid falling into the trap of the Hollywood syndrome again, Van Peebles decided that his next film venture would be independent. He said that one morning he looked in the mirror and said, "You think you're a studio. Therefore, you *are* a studio." Beginning with the $70,000 he had earned on *Watermelon Man,* he set about the enormous task of borrowing the rest of the money he needed to start *Sweet Sweetback.* The story of the actual filming was so dramatic that Van Peebles has published a vivid account in a book entitled *The Making of Sweet Sweetback's Baadasssss Song.* Of the book the *Chicago Tribune* said, "Something new and something very good from story conception to theatre exhibition. A saga with enough technical information to fascinate the most educated in film production."

When *Sweetback* opened at the Grand Circus Theatre in Detroit on March 31, 1971, it set an all-time house record and grossed $45,534 within five days. Following another smashing success in Atlanta, it was brought into New York where it was greeted by an unfavorable review by Roger Greenspun in *The New York Times*. Said he: "I think that Melvin Van Peebles has the talent, the intelligence and even the instincts of a good filmmaker—despite a growing body of evidence to the contrary. The latest exhibit, 'Sweet Sweetback's Baadasssss Song, Van Peebles' third and worst feature, opened yesterday at the Art and Cinerama theaters, and at the Loew's Victoria."

On its Sunday feature pages, *The New York Times* simultaneously printed essays on the film by the white critic Vincent Canby and the black critic Clayton Riley. Canby concluded, "It may be—as some of its supporters claim—the Black Experience in America, distilled to its essence. My feeling, distilled to its essence, is that that experience deserves a better film." Riley commented, ". . . bearing witness to his film is like staring at a Black key sliding through the cosmos, turning sturdy locks and letting out weird figurines to scatter among us."

Throughout the nation in both black and white press, controversies began to rage about the values of the film, and this caused the public to rush to the nearest box office to see what the fuss was all about. According to Van Peebles, the film, which cost only $500,000 to make, grossed around ten million dollars. Says he, "It made five million before three white people had seen it. The real message of 'Sweetback' is that we have the key to our own box office. It's the black dollars, the disenfranchised dollars, that go to see those products."

Van Peebles' next venture was his Broadway production,

Ain't Supposed to Die a Natural Death, which opened in the fall of 1971 with a reported advance sale of nine dollars. It was a sort of panorama of life in the black ghetto ungarnished, really "like it is." There were a series of striking vignettes of the lives of individual characters which anyone who has lived in such an area might recognize all too painfully. At its climax, the author parades these characters around a maypole as if to fix them permanently in our imagination. While this is going on, an old woman comes forward and lays a curse on the audience.

Veteran critic of *The New York Times* Clive Barnes said, "Whites can only treat *Ain't Supposed to Die a Natural Death* as a journey to a foreign country, and on those terms I think it has the power to shock and excite. . . . Passion—sometimes clumsy, sometimes mawkish, sometimes violent—but passion is what Melvin Van Peebles' play is all about. It held me and it pained me. I can forgive its faults, if it can forgive mine."

Because of the highly competitive nature of the commercial theatre, nothing less than solid rave notices can lure regular theatergoers from their comfortable homes in Westchester and other suburbs into the jungle which Broadway has become. Knowing this, Van Peebles began an intensive public relations campaign into the very ghettoes about which his play was concerned and eventually lured enough people into the theatre to keep his work alive. The author told one reporter, "Forty percent of the people who come to my work have never been in the theatre before."

Once Van Peebles was assured that an audience was building for his work, he brought to Broadway still another show in May of 1972 under the title *Don't Play Us Cheap*. The story concerned itself with two demons—a cockroach and a rat—who decide to invade a Saturday night party in Harlem and try to undermine the fun. According to the *Amsterdam News* critic, Lee Cook, "Broadway shook and trembled as the social truth, the knife-like joyous realism of perhaps Black America's premiere artist-playwright extraordinaire, tapped the pulse of an audience which became drunk and delirious with the enthusiasm of its own self-awareness."

Despite herculean public relations efforts, neither of Van Peebles' stage works managed to become a box-office success. More important, however, is that he brought to the stage images with which the black community can immediately identify. He has also given jobs to many talented blacks in all areas of theatrical endeavor from performing to managing. And he has begun to tap a new audience for legitimate theatre which might someday be the shot in the arm that a very sick Broadway needs to revitalize itself.

As to his future plans, Van Peebles is reluctant to commit himself. He once told a reporter, "I can't say because I don't want to intimidate me. There are so many things I'd like to do. Working on a product from one end to another takes about a year every time. After each one of these things, there's a big council meeting inside my head. The council is convening these days. Everyone is screaming, 'Me next!'."

BEN VEREEN
Broadway Musical Star

Although he was born in Miami, Florida, Ben Vereen grew up in Brooklyn, where he began his early training in a neighborhood dancing school. His first professional engagement was in the Vinnette Carroll production of Langston Hughes's gospel song-play, *The Prodigal Son,* off-Broadway. He appeared with Juliet Prowse in the Las Vegas production of *Sweet Charity,* with Shirley MacLaine in the film version, and with Sammy Davis, Jr., in the Chicago and London productions of *Golden Boy.* On the West Coast, he appeared in *Hair* and Charles Gordone's drama *No Place to Be Somebody.* On Broadway, he was nominated for a Tony Award as best supporting actor for his performance as Judas in the musical *Jesus Christ Superstar* and in 1973 he won the Tony Award as best actor in a musical for *Pippin.* In this conversation, which took place in his dressing room at the Imperial Theatre, Vereen discusses his early years, the conflicts between his religious and theatrical interests, and some of the fascinating things that happened to him on the way up to stardom.

ABDUL: When did you start preparing for a career in the performing arts?

VEREEN: I didn't really. I started out as a dancing school

child. My mother sent me to a neighborhood talent school.

ABDUL: Where was that?

VEREEN: In Brooklyn. When I was about ten years old, there were some fellows on the street looking for kids to audition for a neighborhood talent school and I went with about nine hundred other kids in one class—you know—it was one of those rip-off community things. They'd have one teacher who would teach singing and you'd be sitting there with your sheet music and there would be maybe ten or twenty kids lined up on the wall and each one would go up and sing a song and that would be your singing lesson. Then they'd give tap lessons the same way, and at the end of the year they would give a recital. There would be all the mothers and thousands of kids at the Brooklyn Academy in those black silk shirts and blue silk pants with silver tap shoes. That's the type of school I went to.

ABDUL: Did you sing in the church choir?

VEREEN: No, I sang *solo*. I was picked up out of the street by my godmother—a lady by the name of Mary Eddy, who was married to a minister. He had about five old women and his wife who would travel around with him and a group of kids, and he'd go to various churches and preach. Mrs. Eddy would go out on the streets and find kids who weren't in church and I was one of the kids that she found. She is responsible for starting me to sing, because she would teach me a song and then say, "Get out there and sing it!"

ABDUL: So you've had show business in your blood for a long time?

VEREEN: It's funny. I never really recognized it at the time because I thought of the church as being something else other than of the world. I was from a sort of Pentecostal sort of background and this—what I do now is considered worldliness—this is the *Devil's* work and the church is *God's* work. You never looked upon what you did in church as expressing yourself through your art.

ABDUL: Later, while you were a student at the High School of the Performing Arts, you met Vinnette Carroll, who gave you the opportunity to play your first professional show. How did that come about?

VEREEN: Well, when I was doing the senior class dance concert, Vinnette was in the audience. She was teaching in the drama department, and she approached me and said, "I'm doing *The Prodigal Son* off-Broadway and I would love for you to do the lead, but we've already cast the part and we're into rehearsals. I'd love for you to come in and be the understudy and play a small part in it."

ABDUL: Did you consider that experience invaluable?

VEREEN: Yes. Vinnette planted the seed, you know. She used to spend a lot of time saying things to me that I really didn't understand at that time, but today I do—about performing and projection. At that time I was going through the transition of tearing from the church and going into theater.

ABDUL: What did you do after *The Prodigal Son?*

VEREEN: After the *Prodigal,* I kind of felt like I was a failure in my pursuit in the theater and so I decided to go into the ministry. I studied at the Manhattan Institute Theological Seminary, but I found a lot of hypocrisy and I just couldn't put the two together. What I really wanted to do was to perform. One day, I went by to see some of my old classmates and my old teacher, Lester Wilson, who was in *Golden Boy* at the time. I went backstage neatly dressed with my attaché case. I told Lester I was studying to be a minister and he got very uptight because he had spent a lot of time teaching me and he felt that all that time had gone to waste. He gave me Arthur Mitchell's telephone number and said, "Now you call him tomorrow, and don't you let me hear of you going back to that crazy place where you've been going." Arthur was putting together a company to go to Dakar, Senegal.

ABDUL: Did you get to go with them?

VEREEN: No, we didn't get to go to Dakar. Everything fell apart because the government grant didn't come through.

ABDUL: What did you do then?

VEREEN: Ray Cooper called me and said he was doing *West Side Story* and he needed a male dancer. So I went to a little town called Tannersville, Pennsylvania.

ABDUL: Where you became a Puerto Rican.

VEREEN: Right, I played Chico. I started out to do one part, but he was impressed and asked me to stay for the whole summer.

ABDUL: Was this an interracial company?

VEREEN: *I* was the interracial in the company!

ABDUL: What did you do after that summer?

VEREEN: I came back to New York unemployed. I had sublet my place to a friend who didn't pay the rent and I had been evicted from my apartment. I had no money, so I would climb in the fire escape and sleep in my bed at night—they had changed the lock on the door. Then I had all my furniture moved out and avoided the landlord that way. It was suitcase in hand for me.

ABDUL: One of the shows that you did after that lean period was the Chicago and London company of *Golden Boy* with Sammy Davis, Jr. You were an understudy to one of the leads. Did you ever get to go on?

VEREEN: One day Sammy got sick in the middle of a performance in Chicago. The announcer went out and said, "Sammy Davis has just taken ill and will not be able to continue the performance. Lonnie Satin will be playing the part of Joe Wellington [Davis's role] and Ben Vereen will be going on for Lonnie Satin." So I went upstairs to the dressing room and put together my first character.

ABDUL: How long did you have to get yourself together?

VEREEN: Within fifteen minutes. So I went upstairs and sat there and I said—where does this man come from—what am I about? And I really got deep into the character.

ABDUL: That must have been the quickest characterization put together in the history of theatre.

VEREEN: The curtain came up and I had to open the scene. I found myself easing into the character and I looked up for a quick moment across the stage and there was Sammy. He took a stool and sat in the wings and watched me. The character was working—everything worked. When the curtain came down, I got an ovation. When I came offstage, Sammy walked up to me and said, "I'm not going to say anything, because I knew it all the time!"

ABDUL: What was your first Broadway show?

VEREEN: It was *Jesus Christ Superstar*. The producers wanted another person for the role of Judas, but Tom O'Horigan wanted someone who could dance and sing as well—and act well—to bring out the Judas he wanted. He fought for me and I got the role.

ABDUL: You were nominated for a Tony Award for your role in *Jesus Christ Superstar*, were you not?

VEREEN: Yes, but I didn't win. But I *felt* like a winner. I went through the whole ceremony—tense, with worry beads—and then they announced the winner—Larry Blyden. I just sighed and went to the ball afterward and I was so happy and *up*. People came up to me and said, "Gee, I'm sorry you didn't get the Tony." I said: "Oh, but you don't understand—I did!" I was happy just to be nominated.

ABDUL: It was right after the Tony ceremonies that you were called to audition for *Pippin*?

VEREEN: Yes, and I was fresh. I went to the audition feeling good. And I saw Bob Fosse, whom I hadn't seen in six years. He looked up and said, "You gonna sing for me?" I said, "I sure am." And I sang and sang. And I ended up working with Bob again and it was beautiful. I came in like a steam engine ready to work and he said, "Cool it. Lay back—everything's going to be all right—just relax." In *Superstar* everything I did was like—well, I was working—but my energies were dispersed all over the place.

ABDUL: You had to learn to keep something in reserve.

VEREEN: Right. Now I'm working on focus and control. I'm working on just settling back and trusting myself as a performer.

ABDUL: When you do a performance of *Pippin*—you are so highly charged with energy—do you find yourself exhausted after it's over?

VEREEN: That's exactly what I'm talking about. That's what I'm working on.

ABDUL: What do you do to unwind after the show?

VEREEN: I sit here and listen to music for a while after the show. Then I go out and sit around with friends. If I find out that someone's in town recording, then I go over to the studio and sit around and listen. Then I go home and read a bit and crash out.

ABDUL: How did you feel when you finally got the Tony Award as best actor in a musical for *Pippin*?

VEREEN: I felt good. I felt like a winner, you know?

ABDUL: How did your mother react when you told her?

VEREEN: She just said, "That's nice. That's nice!"

ABDUL: What kind of future do you project for yourself in the theatre?

VEREEN: I want to do everything. I'm working right now on my acting, singing, and dancing. And, I'd like to do something straight and some clubs and concerts. But my main objective is to choreograph and direct. I'd like to put a whole show together some day.

ABDUL: Do you honestly think that you could sit there and not want to jump up on the stage and do it yourself?

VEREEN: I'm sure I could.

ABDUL: How do you feel about the opportunities for black performers on the musical stage?

VEREEN: To tell you the truth, I really feel that you can't keep true talent down—no matter what the system or how anybody tries to oppress it—it's always going to come through. Someone's going to recognize you—*you* are going to recognize you—and you're going to keep doing it. I really believe that.

ANDRÉ WATTS
Concert Pianist

"A KEYBOARD ATHLETE of undisputed superiority, he is now at the height of his muscular power and has, in addition, the right combination of looks, charm and hint of mystery to qualify as an ideal American hero." These lines, which recently appeared in *The New York Times* refer to André Watts, who, at the age of sixteen, became the first black instrumental soloist since the turn of the century to appear with the New York Philharmonic Orchestra.

Up to this time, the doors which led to the stages of major concert halls throughout the world were closed tight to the black instrumental soloist. Once in a while they were cracked open for just a fleeting moment to admit one of the handful of extraordinarily gifted artists to make an occasional appearance under the baton of some benevolent conductor. But in spite of what might have been a great success at that moment, no concert manager would risk the perils of trying to build a career for one of these artists. So, soon after the rare moment, stage doors would snap shut as tightly as before.

On January 31, 1963, a miracle occurred in the world of "classical" music. Sixteen-year-old André Watts, an unknown young black pianist, walked out on the stage at

Philharmonic Hall to play the Liszt E Flat Concerto with the New York Philharmonic Orchestra under Leonard Bernstein. As soon as the notes of the final cadenza sounded the audience broke out into an ovation which lasted almost fifteen minutes. And the echoes of this applause resounded via the press throughout the world.

In the Western Edition of *The New York Times* critic Ross Parmenter wrote, "After the opening display of power there came a ravishing modulation to poetic lyricism. The young man made the ensuing gentle passages sing exquisitely." Soon after, *Time* and *Newsweek* devoted columns heralding the coming of this new artist-hero. As if by magic, the doors to every major concert manager's office as well as the previously unfriendly stage doors of symphony orchestras were not only unlocked, but propped open.

In reality, it was not magic alone that created this moment. There was careful manipulation on the part of the shrewd, professional Leonard Bernstein, one of the most powerful figures on the American symphonic scene. Glenn Gould was originally scheduled to play with the orchestra, but fell ill a few days before. André Watts had recently created a sensation on the nationally televised "Young People's Concerts" of the Philharmonic, and fan mail was flooding into the offices of CBS. Nevertheless, it took a lot of hard thinking before Bernstein could justify giving such an important assignment on the Philharmonic's regular subscription series to a youngster with so little performing experience.

After the concert in an interview Bernstein said, "Normally, I would never do such a thing. After all, he's just a boy, just a high school boy. But he's not just another great young pianist. The point is that he's one of those special giants. The seeds of his gianthood are already there. So it seemed a shame not to give him a chance. He just walked right out there like a Persian prince and played it. One day he'll undoubtedly be one of a very special dozen of the world's top pianists."

Much to the credit of both his newly acquired manager and his mother, there was no great effort to cash in on André's sudden rise to fame at the risk of what could be a long-term career. After much deliberation, it was agreed upon that André would play only six concerts the first year, twelve the following, and fifteen the next. And, he would record the Liszt Concerto for Columbia Records so that the world could share this great moment. No sooner had the ink dried on the contracts than the Wattses returned to Philadelphia. André had to go back to his academic and musical studies.

Born on June 20, 1947, in Nuremberg, Germany, André is the son of an Afro-American father and a Hungarian mother. His father, Sergeant Herman Watts, was stationed in Germany when he married Maria Alexandra Gusmits. With the exception of one year when his father was assigned to a post in Philadelphia, André spent his first eight years on army posts in Germany. His musical training began at the age of four, when he began to play a miniature violin. By the age of six, he showed a preference for the piano and began lessons with his mother, an accomplished pianist in her own right. He recalls, "Soon I knew I preferred the piano. I had the hands for it and I was more at home at the keyboard."

When André was eight, his father was transferred back to the United States and the family settled down in Philadelphia. He was enrolled in an academic school as well as in the city's famous Academy of Music. Besides keeping up with his regular school work, he managed to find time to practice the piano about four hours a day. His progress was so phenomenal that, by the time he was nine, he won a competition over forty other gifted youngsters. The prize was an engagement with the Philadelphia Orchestra at its Children's Concerts. This began a long and ardent love affair between the orchestra and André, which continues to this day.

During his school years in Philadelphia, André did not feel that he belonged to any particular race. He was regularly "called out" by his classmates and beaten up after school, but he insists that this was not because he was black or played the piano. It simply happened to everybody. The Irish boys fought the Italian boys and the black boys fought them both. He found a solution to the problem of coping with this situation by teaching himself a little judo. Soon the beatings stopped.

Eventually, André's parents divorced. André always respected his father and remembers him as "a damn good soldier" who always wore amazingly shiny shoes and had his own system of ethics. He believed that if a relationship came to an end, then it should be finished without regrets. It is in this spirit that André accepted his father's departure from the household, and he hasn't heard from him since.

André and his mother moved into an unusual little three-story house with only one room to a floor and a winding staircase. Because of its peculiar structure, the all-important piano had to be placed on the first floor together with a narrow sofa bed on which André could sleep. To make sure that André could develop his talents fully, Mrs. Watts created an isolated little world around him. She did everything she could to supply her son with the emotional security factors so necessary in the life of an artist.

After he completed his studies in Philadelphia, André did advanced work with Leon Fleisher at the Peabody Conservatory, from which he eventually was graduated. At that time, André told one reporter, "Maintaining school and concerts during the season is a problem. I've tried to study on planes and in hotel rooms, but I like to concentrate on one thing at a time and cannot do both. So I've worked out my schedule so that I do five dates and come back to school work."

Of his work with Fleisher, André says, "The biggest tribute to him—and the most beautiful thing—is that when I first came to him, he told me what the position of a teacher is. He told me to bring him a piece of music and, with it, several possibilities and ideas for the music. 'The ideal way,' he said 'is that you have your own ideas and then I give you mine. Then you can see them all in front of you and finally evolve your own way and your own manner in the end.'"

Before a pianist can consider himself a complete artist, he must prove himself in a *solo* recital. At this moment, he must walk out on a bare stage with only a piano, a spotlight and the total sum of his own musical personality. The auditorium is filled with experts (critics and other pianists) and a discriminating public used to hearing the world's greatest artists. They are waiting to analyze every musical phrase. The pianist is, in the phrase beautifully coined by *The New York Times* feature writer Joan Barthel, "on the threshold of the big plunge."

For André, this moment came on October 26, 1966, at Philharmonic Hall, where his New York debut recital was placed daringly within the framework of the Great Performers Series. Of this event Harold C. Schonberg, the chief critic of *The New York Times,* reported, ". . . He has the power of communication and the audience loved what it heard. This kind of pianistic, as opposed to musical authority is rare from one of Mr. Watts's years, even considering the general high level of piano playing today. May his artistry also develop in line with such a natural gift." Another distinguished critic, Winthrop Sargeant of the *New Yorker* Magazine found André "a bravura pianist of stunning achievements and a romantic pianist whose style takes one back to the great days of men like Moriz Rosenthal."

Of the act of performing, André told one writer, "My greatest satisfaction is performing. The ego is a big part of it, but far from all. Performing is my way of being part of humanity—of sharing. I don't want to play for a few people, I want to play for thousands. . . . There's something beautiful about having an entire audience hanging on a single note. I'd rather have a standing ovation than have some chick come backstage and tell me how great I was. When people come around after a concert it's less pleasant, because they're trying to get a piece of me."

At the present time, André lives in New York, just a

stone's throw from Carnegie Hall. Both he and his mother
have separate apartments in the same building. His apartment has high ceilings with an attractive molding setting
off the white walls. The sitting room has a black leather
sofa and bookshelves crammed with books and record albums. There is an artificial tree and a steel sculpture with
running water entitled *The Bird of Paradise* (a gift from his
mother). There are portraits of Liszt and Beethoven and
two busts of Liszt. And, in the place of honor, a Baldwin
piano.

When André is not on tour, his day usually begins
around 8 A.M. with Yoga exercises, shower, and breakfast
of orange juice, raw egg yolks, corn flakes, and coffee. He
usually practices from nine or ten until noon with a break
for lunch and a short nap. This is followed by more Yoga
and practice at the piano until seven in the evening. He
usually eats dinner with his mother. He rarely goes out
and dislikes parties, because they are "a great waste of life
force." Instead, he spends his evenings chatting with a few
friends or reading musical scores and books.

Over a period of ten short years, André has become
what is known in the music business as "one of the hottest
properties." This means he plays almost one hundred
dates a year and commands a fee of about $6,000 per con-
cert. He is booked around the world for three seasons
ahead. One of the highlights of his career is that he was
chosen to be the first American pianist to play in Red
China—as soloist with the Philadelphia Orchestra.

FLIP WILSON
Comedian-Television Star

"What a dull and heavy creature," said a Hare, "is this Tortoise." "And yet," said the Tortoise, "I'll run with you for a wager." So it was done. And the Fox, it was decided by mutual consent, would be the Judge. They started together and the Tortoise kept jogging along until he came to the end of the course. The Hare stopped about midway and took a nap. "For," said he, "I can catch up with the Tortoise when I please." But he overslept and when he finally awakened, though he ran as fast as possible, the Tortoise reached the post before him and won the wager.

—an Aesop fable

"My progress has been like that of the tortoise in Aesop's fable—'slowly but surely wins the race!' However, the race is never really over unless you quit," says Flip Wilson, whose television series "The Flip Wilson Show" on NBC has risen to the top of the popularity charts. And, like the black fabulist, Aesop, Flip Wilson is a master of humorous commentary on the human condition.

Actually, Flip's beginning in the race for success in show business began at the age of nine, when he was given a small part in a school play about the famous nurse Clara Barton. At the last minute, the girl who was supposed to play Clara got sick and Flip (then Clerow) was the only one who knew all the lines. So he got the part. Flip recalls, "I didn't decide right then and there to go into show business. I enjoyed making the other kids laugh and it was also rather easy for me, but show business was not on my mind. I used my natural voice for Clara Barton. I didn't try to sound like a girl or anything. Just having that many lines was enough of a thrill for me, because, until then, I was just going to be a wounded soldier in the play with nothing to do but groan."

Young Flip began sneaking into the old Mosque Theatre in Jersey City to watch the vaudeville stars performing their routines. As the waves of laughter greeted their antics, Flip found the whole thing quite magical. He doesn't remember exactly who the comics were. Possibly they were Stump and Stumpy. Nevertheless, he began to feel that he could make people laugh too. Visions of being up on that stage began to dance through his head.

"I used to take fantasy trips into the soap operas on radio and into my favorite comic strips 'Captain Marvel' and 'Little Orphan Annie,' " he recalls. "Sometimes, Little Orphan Annie was too sad for me. I doubt if I ever finished an episode of it, because I guess I felt too much identification with her. When things got tough, I'd stop reading until it all came out all right."

It is easy to understand how Flip got caught up in a world of fantasy, because life at home was concerned mostly with survival. He was one of twenty-four children. His mother abandoned the family when Flip was still a youngster and his father, who was a carpenter, always had difficulty finding work. They would float from place to place in search of rentals they could afford. Finally, the authorities placed Flip in various foster homes. Again and again he would run away, so he was sent to reform school. It was there that one of his happiest childhood memories took place. His teacher gave him a package containing a box of Cracker Jack and a can of A.B.C. shoe polish for his birthday.

When Flip was sixteen, he pushed his age up a few notches and joined the Air Force. Ashamed of his shabby clothes, he felt that the Air Force beat parking cars for a living. Although at first he was assigned like most blacks to kitchen duty, a Southern white major persuaded him to learn typing and grammar, which he did with great success. During his spare time, he began entertaining the other guys with funny stories. His pals used to say "He's flipped," and soon he acquired the nickname "Flip."

When he left the service at the age of twenty, Flip took a job as a forty-dollars-a-week bellhop in a San Francisco hotel. At that time an adagio dance trio was performing at the hotel and Flip got his first professional break in show business when he filled in with a drunk routine while the trio changed costumes. The customers liked his act, so he was invited by the dancers to join the troupe on their tour at the startling fee of one dollar a night.

When the dancers completed their engagement at the hotel, Flip quit his job as bellhop and joined them on their tour of obscure California night spots. In one town the hotel room cost the performers more than they had earned, so, during the wee hours of the morning, they tossed their luggage from the fire escape into the back seat of their battered convertible and made an inexpensive exit. After he left them, Flip continued playing small clubs around the country on his own. "Those black audiences in the little weekend clubs were the toughest I've ever played for," he recalls. "With all the trouble black people have, they try to forget on weekends. You've got to be good to make them laugh."

In 1965, while Flip was playing in a small Miami club, a local white businessman saw enough promise in the young performer to offer him a subsidy of fifty dollars a week for a year so that he could take time to write some comedy scripts and develop his act. Of great influence in his life at this time was Max Eastman's book, *Enjoyment of Laughter*, an analysis of what makes people laugh. Eventually he began to compile his own book, entitled *Flip's Laws of Comedy*, in which he carefully typed out his own personal observations.

Flip's first exposure to national television audiences came about when Redd Foxx was asked by Johnny Carson on "The Tonight Show" who he considered the funniest comedian around. Redd replied, "Flip Wilson." Carson invited Flip to appear on his show and he broke everyone up with a sketch about a black woman buying a wig. After trying on several, she turned to the salesman and asked, "You sure it don't make me look too Polish?"

On another "Tonight Show" appearance, Flip was seen in one of his classic routines—Columbus and Isabella. In trying to get Isabella to provide money for his first trip to America, Columbus tells her that, without America, there would be no Ray Charles. "You gonna find Ray Charles?" screeches the Queen. After writing him out a check to buy the *Pinta,* the *Nina,* and the *Santa Maria* at the local Army and Navy store, Isabella announces to the crowd, "Chris goin' to America on that boat. Chris goin' to find Ray Charles!" This unique interpretation of a historic event took Flip three years to develop.

After numerous guest shots on such shows as "Laugh-In," "Carol Burnett," and "Dean Martin," Flip was offered an NBC special of his own. Finding the right format was not an easy task. The first attempt taped in 1968 remains on the shelf to this day. But patience and continued hard work resulted in his famous 1969 special, which introduced a startled America to his famous character Geraldine. Officials at NBC were so impressed that they signed Flip to a contract for his own show for the coming season.

When "The Flip Wilson Show" finally made its way to television screens, Geraldine's famous lines "What you see is what you get!" and "Don't fight the feelin'" echoed and reechoed from coast to coast. At one point, it was reported by Nielsen that the program reached 40,000,000 viewers. Flip's reaction was, "It means I have to work as hard as I can to entertain those forty million people. If I were to fail to try, it would mean that my neglect wasted forty million hours—that's eighty lifetimes—enough time to find cures for cancer, heart disease, sickle-cell anemia, and war. I have to work!"

During the twenty-six weeks of the year when the show is being taped, Flip leads the life of a monk. He is seldom seen at parties and has very few friends in Hollywood. Preparation for the show begins each Monday with a reading of the script and judicious editing by Flip himself. Rehearsals begin on Tuesday, followed by a general run-through on Wednesday and a camera blocking on Thursday. On Friday there is a dress rehearsal and a final taping at 8:00 P.M. Both the rehearsal and show are taped before a live audience, with the best scenes being spliced together for broadcast the following week.

Although his yearly earnings are reported to be well over $1,000,000, Flip lives in a rented house in Hollywood Hills and allows himself only a few luxuries. One of these is his ice-blue Rolls-Royce with a license plate marked KILLER and equipped with stereo, Dunhill pipe rack, and a mobile telephone. Quite often, to relax, he will take a spin to the desert armed with a note pad and pencil. He says, "I don't go to create, I go to relax. But I've never gone and not come back with something—a couple of stories, a handful of one-liners."

He seems to enjoy popping up in unexpected places. Once he received a fan letter from a teen-age girl which related how much her mother liked Flip's show and how her mother would like to meet him. She enclosed a copy of a book her mother had written. Flip decided to drive over to San Diego and appear unannounced at their home. "I just walked up to the door and rang the bell," he relates. "The door was open and the lady, when she saw me through the screen door, said, 'Flip Wilson, what are you doing here?' I explained about her daughter's letter and we just chatted about twenty minutes and then I returned to Los Angeles."

Anyone who tries to get a glimpse into the private world of Flip Wilson meets with an immediate impasse. When confronted with questions of a personal nature by a leading magazine writer he said, "My show is my statement.

What I have to say is on the screen. My life is my own. I don't want to talk about my private self. Why should I?" In the words of his famous character Geraldine, "What you see, honey, is what you get!"

INDEX

INDEX

INDEX

156

INDEX

INDEX

INDEX

ABOUT THE AUTHOR

Raoul Abdul has distinguished himself both in the fields of literature and entertainment. After serving many years as the literary assistant to the late Langston Hughes, he co-edited (with Alan Lomax) the classic anthology *Three Thousand Years of Black Poetry* and edited *The Magic of Black Poetry*. His theatrical training started in the Children's Theatre of the Cleveland Play House, where his colleagues included Joel Grey and Joan Diener. But it was his appearances in operatic productions at Karamu Theatre which led to study at the Vienna Academy of Music and Dramatic Art and a career as a concert singer.